BIRDS
of
BOSTON

Chris C. Fisher
Andy Bezener

LONE
PINE

The Publisher: Lone Pine Publishing

1901 Raymond Ave. SW, Suite C	206, 10426 – 81 Ave.	202A, 1110 Seymour St.
Renton, WA 98055	Edmonton, AB T6E 1X5	Vancouver, BC V6B 3N3
USA	Canada	Canada

Lone Pine Publishing website: http://www.lonepinepublishing.com

Canadian Cataloguing in Publication Data

Fisher, Chris C. (Christopher Charles), (date)
    Birds of Boston

    Includes bibliographical references and index.
    ISBN 1-55105-182-6

    1. Birds—Massachusetts—Boston—Identification. 2. Bird watching—Massachusetts—Boston. I. Bezener, Andy, (date) II. Title.
QL684.M4F57 1998   598'.09744'61   C98-910091-X

Senior Editor: Nancy Foulds
Project Editor: Roland Lines
Production Manager: David Dodge
Layout and Production: Michelle Bynoe
Cartography: Volker Bodegom
Cover Design: Michelle Bynoe
Cover Illustration: Gary Ross
Illustrations: Gary Ross, Ted Nordhagen, Ewa Pluciennik
Technical Review: Greg Butcher
Separations and Film: Elite Lithographers Co., Edmonton, Alberta
Printing: Quality Colour Press, Edmonton, Alberta

The publisher gratefully acknowledges the assistance of the Department of Canadian Heritage.

Contents

Acknowledgments

A book such as this is made possible by the inspired work of Boston's naturalist community, whose contributions continue to advance the science of ornithology and to motivate a new generation of nature lovers.

Our thanks go to Gary Ross and Ted Nordhagen, whose illustrations have elevated the quality of this book; to the birding societies of the Boston area, which all make daily contributions to natural history; to Carole Patterson and Kindrie Grove, for their continual support; to the team at Lone Pine Publishing—Roland Lines, Nancy Foulds, Eloise Pulos, Greg Brown, Michelle Bynoe and Shane Kennedy—for their input and steering; to John Acorn and Jim Butler, for their stewardship and their remarkable passion; and to Wayne Campbell, a premier naturalist whose works have served as models of excellence.

This book would not have been possible without the assistance of Greg Butcher, the executive director of the American Birding Association. He has a lifetime of birding experience from across the Americas, and his familiarity with birding in the Boston area was an invaluable resource.

Introduction

No matter where we live, birds are a natural part of our lives. We are so used to seeing them that we often take their presence for granted, but when we take the time to notice their colors, songs and behaviors, we experience their dynamic appeal.

This book presents a brief introduction into the lives of birds. It is intended to serve as both a bird identification guide and a bird appreciation guide. Getting to know the names of birds is the first step toward getting to know birds. Once we've made contact with a species, we can better appreciate its character and mannerisms during future encounters. Over a lifetime of meetings, many birds become acquaintances, some seen daily, others not for years.

The selection of species within this book represents a balance between the familiar and the noteworthy. Many of the 127 species described in this guide are the most common species found in the Boston area. Others are less common, but they are noteworthy because they are important ecologically or because their particular status grants them a high profile. It would be impossible for a beginners' book such as this to comprehensively describe all the birds found in the Boston area. Furthermore, there is no one site where all the species within this book can be observed simultaneously, but most species can be viewed—at least seasonally—within a short drive (or sail) from Boston.

It is hoped that this guide will inspire novice birdwatchers into spending some time outdoors, gaining valuable experience with the local bird community. This book stresses the identity of birds, but it also attempts to bring them to life by discussing their various character traits. We often discuss these traits in human terms, because personifying a bird's character can help us to feel a bond with the birds. The perceived links with birds should not be mistaken for actual behaviors, however, because our interpretations can falsely reflect the complexities of bird life.

FEATURES OF THE LANDSCAPE

Few cities are as rich and diverse in bird life as Boston. In the early days of ornithological study, Boston became one of the finest birdwatching regions in the country, and it continues to fascinate researchers and birding enthusiasts alike. The Boston area is strategically located within a major north-south bird migration path known as the Atlantic Flyway. Tens of thousands of birds pass through our city each year, and the local preserves and sanctuaries support these numbers. Despite the ever-increasing demand for urban development, hundreds of acres of protected woodlands, bays, beaches and harbors ensure the continued abundance of bird life.

The marine environment supports a wide variety of birds, and all seasons have their specialties. During peak migratory periods, large numbers of migrant birds—ducks, gulls, terns and shorebirds—congregate along our sandy shorelines to replenish their energy supplies, slowly moving from one productive foraging site to another. Wintering birds, such as ducks and gulls, feed on the plant and animal life that can be found along our shorelines, and during the breeding season, species such as the Piping Plover and Least Tern nest along gravel beaches. There are endless possibilities for Massachusetts birders, but one spot not to miss is the Parker River National Wildlife Refuge in Essex County—saltmarshes, sand dunes and vast stretches of beach make it a rich haven for birds any time of the year.

The open waters off coastal Massachusetts are particularly productive, and, with the exception of the summer breeding season, always host great rafts of seabirds. Areas such as Nahant in Boston Harbor North or Wollaston Beach in Quincy Bay can be especially viable throughout the winter months. Large numbers of waterfowl, such as Greater Scaups and Common Eiders, often winter here, along with loons and grebes. Boston's extensive collection of offshore islands are also preferred habitat for many birds. Many migrants find comfortable refuge along their rocky shores, and during the summer months, species such as the Snowy Egret nest there in colonies.

The inland ponds, freshwater marshes and river meadows of the Sudbury River valley offer some of the most productive birding habitat in the state. Within a short commuting distance, this area will inevitably offer rewarding birding opportunities—species such as the Virginia Rail and the Marsh Wren are regularly seen and heard among the marshland cattails, and it is also possible to spot land birds roaming through nearby fields or pastures. With the rate of urban development and the slow disappearance of Massachusetts's wetlands, areas such as these have become increasingly

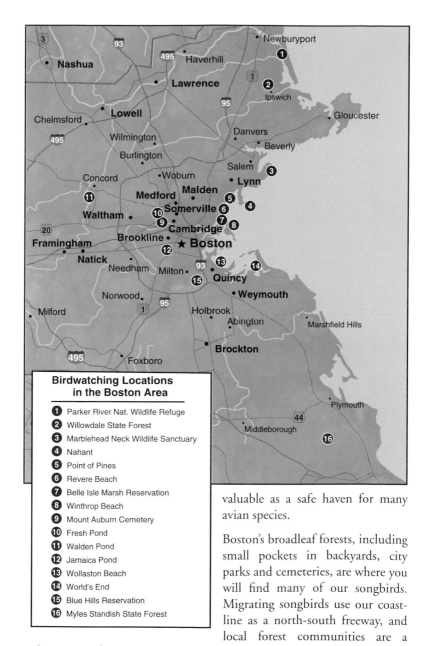

Birdwatching Locations in the Boston Area

1. Parker River Nat. Wildlife Refuge
2. Willowdale State Forest
3. Marblehead Neck Wildlife Sanctuary
4. Nahant
5. Point of Pines
6. Revere Beach
7. Belle Isle Marsh Reservation
8. Winthrop Beach
9. Mount Auburn Cemetery
10. Fresh Pond
11. Walden Pond
12. Jamaica Pond
13. Wollaston Beach
14. World's End
15. Blue Hills Reservation
16. Myles Standish State Forest

valuable as a safe haven for many avian species.

Boston's broadleaf forests, including small pockets in backyards, city parks and cemeteries, are where you will find many of our songbirds. Migrating songbirds use our coastline as a north-south freeway, and local forest communities are a welcome site for many hungry and tired travelers. Every year, Mount Auburn Cemetery is inundated with thousands of tiny land birds, and it is the site of a spectacular migration display. The beautiful gardens and woodlands of Mount Auburn are renowned statewide as one of the best locations to experience the excitement of the spring passage. If there is opportunity to travel outside Boston, try visiting Willowdale State Forest. Its mixed woods, fields and marshes are favored habitat for migrating birds, and it is a favored nesting spot for many species during the summer months.

The landscaped setting of our city is also a good place to become acquainted with bird life. Backyard feeders are a welcome invitation for many species, and to the delight of area residents, many birds make use of nest boxes during summer. Small city parks and backyards are permanent homes for the Downy Woodpecker, the Blue Jay and the Black-capped Chickadee, but you will also find birds that are exceptionally adapted to urban areas, such as Rock Doves, House Sparrows and European Starlings.

THE IMPORTANCE OF HABITAT

Understanding the relationships between habitats and bird species often helps identify which birds are which. Because you won't find a loon up a tree or a bobwhite out at sea, habitat is an important thing to note when birdwatching.

The quality of habitat is one of the most powerful factors to influence bird distribution, and with experience you might become amazed by the predictability of some birds within a specific habitat type. The habitat icons in this book show where each species is most likely to be seen. It is important to realize, however, that because of their migratory habits, birds are sometimes found in completely different habitats. These unexpected surprises, despite being confusing to novice birders, are among the most powerful motivations for the increasing legion of birdwatchers.

Oceans and Bays

Coastal Shorelines

Estuaries
and Marshes

Rivers, Ponds
and Lakes

Grasslands
and Fields

Thickets, Clearings
and Edges

Woodlands

Parks and
Gardens

THE ORGANIZATION OF THIS BOOK

To simplify field identification, *Birds of Boston* is organized slightly differently from other field guides, many of which use strict phylogenetic groupings. In cases where many birds from the same family are described, conventional groupings are maintained in our book. In other cases, however, distantly related birds that share physical and behavioral similarities are grouped together. This blend of family groupings and groups of physically similar species strives to help the novice birdwatcher identify and appreciate the birds he or she encounters.

DIVING BIRDS

loons, grebes, gannets, cormorants

These heavy-bodied birds are adapted to diving for their food. Between their underwater foraging dives, they are most frequently seen on the surface of the water. These birds could only be confused with one another or with certain diving ducks.

WETLAND WADERS

herons, rails, coots

Although this group varies considerably in size, and represents two separate families of birds, wetland waders share similar habitat and food preferences. Some of these long-legged birds of marshes are quite common, but certain species are heard far more than they are seen.

WATERFOWL

swans, geese, ducks

Waterfowl tend to have stout bodies and webbed feet, and they are swift in flight. Although most species are associated with water, waterfowl can sometimes be seen grazing on upland sites.

VULTURES, HAWKS AND FALCONS

vultures, eagles, hawks, kestrels

From deep forests to open country to large lakes, there are hawks and falcons hunting the skies. Their predatory look—sharp talons, hooked bills and forward-facing eyes—easily identifies members of this group. They generally forage during the day, and hawks and vultures use their broad wings to soar in thermals and updrafts.

QUAILS

The Northern Bobwhite bears a superficial resemblance to a chicken. It is a stout bird and a poor flyer, and it is most often encountered on the ground or when flushed.

SHOREBIRDS

plovers, sandpipers, dowitchers, etc.

Although these small, long-legged, swift-flying birds are mainly found along shores, don't be surprised to find certain species in pastures and marshy areas.

GULLS AND TERNS

Gulls are relatively large, usually light-colored birds that are frequently seen swimming, walking about in urban areas or soaring gracefully over the city. Their backs tend to be darker than their bellies, and their feet are webbed. Terns are in the same grouping as gulls, but they rarely soar and they have straight, pointed bills.

DOVES

Both of Boston's doves are easily recognizable. Rock Doves are found in all urban areas, from city parks to the downtown core, but they have many of the same physical and behavioral characteristics as the 'wilder' Mourning Doves.

NOCTURNAL BIRDS

These night hunters all have large eyes. Owls, which primarily prey on rodents, have powerful, taloned feet and strongly hooked bills. Nighthawks, which catch moths and other nocturnal insects on the wing, have extremely large mouths.

KINGFISHERS

The Belted Kingfisher's behavior and physical characteristics are quite unlike any other bird's in Boston. It primarily hunts fish, plunging after them from the air or from an overhanging perch.

WOODPECKERS

The drumming sound as they hammer wood and their precarious foraging habits easily identify most woodpeckers. They are frequently seen in forests, clinging to trunks and chipping away bark with their straight, sturdy bills. Even when these birds cannot be seen or heard, the characteristic marks of certain species can be seen on trees in any mature forest.

HUMMINGBIRDS

The Ruby-throated Hummingbird is Boston's smallest bird. Its bright colors and swift flight are very characteristic.

FLYCATCHERS

flycatchers, phoebes, kingbirds

These birds might be best identified by their foraging behavior. As their name implies, flycatchers catch insects on the wing, darting after them from a favorite perch. Many flycatchers have subdued plumage, but kingbirds are rather boldly marked.

SWIFTS AND SWALLOWS

Members of these two families are typically seen at their nest sites or in flight. Small and sleek, swallows fly gracefully in pursuit of insects. Swifts are small, dark birds with long, narrow wings and short tails, and they have a more 'mechanical' flight behavior.

JAYS AND CROWS

Many members of this family are known for their intelligence and adaptability. These birds are easily observed, and they are frequently extremely bold, teasing the animal-human barrier. They are some-times called 'corvids,' from Corvidae, the scientific name for the family.

SMALL SONGBIRDS

chickadees, nuthatches, wrens, etc.

Birds in this group are all generally smaller than a sparrow. Many of them associate with one another in mixed-species flocks, and they are commonly encountered in city parks, backyards and other wooded areas.

BLUEBIRDS AND THRUSHES

bluebirds, thrushes, robins

From the bold robin to the secretive forest thrushes, this group of beautiful singers has the finest collective voice. Although some thrushes are very familiar, others require a little experience and patience to identify.

VIREOS AND WARBLERS

vireos, warblers, redstarts, etc.

Vireos tend to dress in pale olive, whereas warblers are splashed liberally with colors. All these birds are very small, however, and they sing characteristic courtship songs.

MID-SIZED SONGBIRDS

tanagers, starlings, waxwings, etc.

The birds within this group are all sized between a sparrow and a robin. Tanagers are very colorful and sing complex, flute-like songs, but waxwings are more reserved in dress and voice. Starlings are frequently seen and heard all over Boston.

SPARROWS

towhees, sparrows, juncos, buntings

These small, often indistinct birds are predominantly brown and streaky. Their songs are often very useful in identification. Many birdwatchers discount sparrows as 'little brown birds'—towhees are colorful exceptions—but they are worthy of the extra identification effort.

BLACKBIRDS AND ORIOLES

blackbirds, cowbirds, orioles, etc.

Most of these birds are predominantly black and have relatively long tails. They are common in open areas, city parks and agricultural fields. The Eastern Meadowlark belongs in the blackbird family despite not being black and having a short tail.

FINCH-LIKE BIRDS

finches, cardinals, grosbeaks, etc.

These finches and finch-like birds are primarily adapted to feeding on seeds, and they have stout, conical bills. Many are birdfeeder regulars, and they are a familiar part of the winter scene.

MEASUREMENTS

The size measurement given for each bird is an average length of the bird from the tip of its bill to the tip of its tail. It is an approximate measurement of the bird as it is seen in nature (rather than a measurement of stuffed specimens, which tend to be straighter and therefore longer).

In many situations, it is more useful to know a bird's comparative size, rather than its actual length in inches, so the 'Quick I.D.' for each species describes the bird's size in relation to a common, well-known bird (e.g., sparrow-sized, smaller than a robin, etc.). It must be remembered that these are general impressions of size that are influenced as much by the bulk of a bird as by its total length.

PLUMAGES

One of the complications to birdwatching is that many species look different in spring and summer than they do in fall and winter—they have what are generally called *breeding* and *non-breeding* plumages—and young birds often look quite different from their parents. This book does not try to describe or illustrate all the different plumages of a species; instead, it focuses on the forms that are most commonly seen in our area. All the illustrations are of adult birds.

ABUNDANCE CHARTS

Accompanying each bird description is a chart that indicates the relative abundance of the species throughout the year. These stylized graphs offer some insight into the distribution and abundance of the birds, but they should not be viewed as definitive—they represent a generalized overview. There could be inconsistencies specific to time and location, but these charts should provide readers with a basic reference for bird abundance and occurrence.

Each chart is divided into the 12 months of the year. The pale orange that colors the chart is an indication of abundance: the higher the color, the more common the bird. Dark orange is used to indicate the nesting period. The time frame is approximate, however, and nesting birds can sometimes be found both before and after the period indicated on the chart. If no nesting color is shown, the bird breeds outside the Boston area or visits Boston in significant numbers during migration or winter.

These graphs are based on personal observations and on local references, including those listed on p. 151.

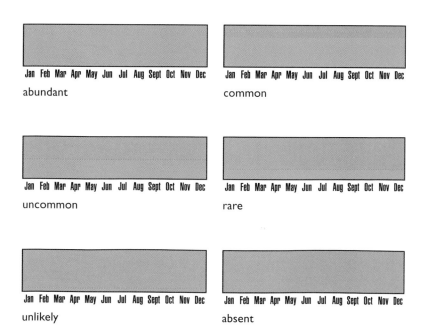

Jan Feb Mar Apr May Jun Jul Aug Sept Oct Nov Dec
abundant

Jan Feb Mar Apr May Jun Jul Aug Sept Oct Nov Dec
common

Jan Feb Mar Apr May Jun Jul Aug Sept Oct Nov Dec
uncommon

Jan Feb Mar Apr May Jun Jul Aug Sept Oct Nov Dec
rare

Jan Feb Mar Apr May Jun Jul Aug Sept Oct Nov Dec
unlikely

Jan Feb Mar Apr May Jun Jul Aug Sept Oct Nov Dec
absent

Common Loon
Gavia immer

The Common Loon is a noble symbol of northern wilderness, preferring the diminishing pristine areas where birds alone quarrel over naval rights-of-way. Loons do not breed in our area, but they visit each year during migration and over winter. In the Boston area, they are most often spotted from Wollaston Beach and World's End in their brown winter plumage as they float serenely upon the waves of Quincy Bay.

Common Loons dive deeply and efficiently, compressing their feathers to reduce underwater drag and to decrease their buoyancy. Propelling themselves primarily with their legs, these heavy birds manage to outswim fish over short distances. Loons have solid bones (unlike most other birds). From his cabin at Walden Pond, Henry David Thoreau wrote of the loon: 'How surprised must fishes be to see this ungainly visitor from another sphere, speeding his way amid their schools.' Thoreau considered its uncommonly heard voice 'perhaps the wildest sound ever heard, ... making the woods ring far and wide.'

Similar Species: Red-throated Loon in winter plumage has white highlights on its back and lacks the dark colors on the side of the neck. Double-crested Cormorant (p. 19) has all-black plumage and a long neck, and it usually holds its bill pointed upward when it swims. Common Merganser has an orange bill and very white sides.

non-breeding

Quick I.D.: larger than a duck; sexes similar; stout, sharp bill. *In flight:* hunch-backed. *Breeding:* dark green hood; black-and-white checkerboard back; fine, white 'necklace.' *Non-breeding:* sandy-brown back; light underparts.
Size: 27–33 in.

Jan Feb Mar Apr May Jun Jul Aug Sept Oct Nov Dec

Horned Grebe
Podiceps auritus

Like many water birds that winter in the Boston area, Horned Grebes lose their splendid summer plumage and assume a low-key, gray-and-white coloring. So dramatic is their transformation, that from their summer wardrobe (seen briefly in March and April before their departure) only their blood red eyes remain. Horned Grebes are common in protected bays and along ocean coasts from October through April. They are commonly seen on Quincy Bay and Nahant Bay. Their behavior is characteristically peppy: they leap up before neatly diving headfirst into the water.

Grebes are an unusual and unique group of birds. They have unusual feet: unlike the fully webbed feet of ducks, gulls, cormorants and alcids, grebes' feet have individually lobed toes. All grebes eat feathers, a seemingly strange habit that frequently causes their digestive systems to become packed. It is thought that this behavior protects their stomachs from sharp fish bones, and it might also slow the passage of the bones through the digestive system so that more nutrients can be digested.

Similar Species: Pied-billed Grebe has a dark neck and underparts and is almost always found in fresh water.

non-breeding

Quick I.D.: smaller than a duck; sexes similar; white cheek; dark crown and upperparts; light underparts; short bill (shorter than head width); red eyes.
Size: 12¹/₂–15 in.

Jan Feb Mar Apr May Jun Jul Aug Sept Oct Nov Dec

Northern Gannet
Morus bassanus

With its long, tapered bill, pointed tail and narrow, black wing tips on an otherwise large, white body, the Northern Gannet is easily identified as the bird that is 'pointed at all ends.' Gannets are renowned for their spectacular feeding behavior, which is uncommonly seen within sight of land. Squadrons of gannets, often soaring more than 100 feet above the ocean surface, will suddenly fold back their wings to stop their flight and then plunge in a stooping, headfirst dive into the ocean depths in pursuit of schooling fish.

This bird is the sole northern relative of the spectacular Blue-footed, Red-footed, Brown and Masked boobies of more southerly tropical seas. Unlike the boobies, which all sport snazzy, colorful feet, the black-footed Northern Gannet spends most of the year feeding and roosting on the open sea. Most gannets leave our area to breed in northern sea-cliff colonies. Your best chance of seeing a gannet is during fall along the outer coast or from a vessel exploring the outer reaches of Massachusetts Bay.

Similar Species: Snow Goose has a shorter, pinkish bill, broader wings and a long, extended neck in flight.

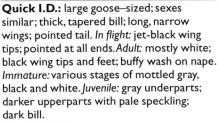

Quick I.D.: large goose–sized; sexes similar; thick, tapered bill; long, narrow wings; pointed tail. *In flight:* jet-black wing tips; pointed at all ends. *Adult:* mostly white; black wing tips and feet; buffy wash on nape. *Immature:* various stages of mottled gray, black and white. *Juvenile:* gray underparts; darker upperparts with pale speckling; dark bill.
Size: 35–38 in.

Jan Feb Mar Apr May Jun Jul Aug Sept Oct Nov Dec

Double-crested Cormorant
Phalacrocorax auritus

When Double-crested Cormorants are seen flying in single-file, low over Boston Harbor, the prehistoric sight hints of their ancestry. The tight, dark flocks soar and sail over the ocean until hunger or the need for rest draws them to the water's surface. It is there that cormorants are most comfortable, disappearing beneath the surface in deep foraging dives.

Cormorants lack the ability to waterproof their feathers, so they need to dry their wings after each swim. They frequently perch on dock pilings and buoys with their wings partially spread to expose their wet feathers to the sun and the wind. It would seem to be a great disadvantage for a water bird to have to dry its wings, but the cormorant's ability to wet its feathers decreases the bird's buoyancy, making it easier for the cormorant to swim after the fish on which it preys. Sealed nostrils, a long, rudder-like tail and excellent underwater vision are other features of the cormorant's aquatic lifestyle.

breeding

Similar Species: Great Cormorant has a white chin strap and white flank patches during the breeding season. Common Loon (p. 16) has a shorter neck and is more stout overall.

Quick I.D.: goose-sized; sexes similar; all black; long tail; long neck. *In flight:* kinked neck; rapid wingbeats. *Breeding:* bright orange throat pouch; black plumes streaming back from eyebrows (seen only at close range). *First year:* brown; pale neck, breast and belly.
Size: 30–35 in.

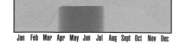

Jan Feb Mar Apr May Jun Jul Aug Sept Oct Nov Dec

Great Blue Heron
Ardea herodias

The Great Blue Heron is one of the largest and most regal birds in our area. It often stands motionless as it surveys the calm waters, its graceful lines blending naturally with the grasses and cattails of wetlands. All herons have specialized vertebrae that enable the neck to fold back over itself. The S-shaped neck, seen in flight, identifies all members of this wading family.

Hunting herons space themselves out evenly in favorite hunting spots, and they will strike out suddenly at prey below the water's surface. In flight, their lazy wingbeats slowly but effortlessly carry them up to their nests. These herons nest communally, high in trees, building bulky stick nests that are easily seen along wooded swamps and beaver ponds west of the Boston area. Although they do not breed in the Boston area, migrating and non-breeding birds can often be seen wading elegantly through the shallows of Fresh Pond, Jamaica Pond and Belle Isle Marsh Reservation.

Similar Species: Great Egret and Snowy Egret (p. 21) are similar to the Great Blue Heron in build, but they are all white, and the Snowy Egret is only half as tall. Black-crowned Night-Heron has a black cap and back.

breeding

Quick I.D.: very large heron; sexes similar; gray-blue plumage; long, dagger-like, yellow bill. *In flight:* eagle-sized wingspan; head folded back; legs held straight back.
Size: 48–52 in.

Jan Feb Mar Apr May Jun Jul Aug Sept Oct Nov Dec

Snowy Egret
Egretta thula

The other herons and egrets that hunt the shallows of Boston Harbor do so in slow, purposeful strides, but the Snowy Egret occasionally chooses a more energetic approach. It stirs the water with its golden slippers—its black legs are tipped with bright yellow toes that glow in the shallow water—to lure small fish, crustaceans and insects into striking range. Alternately, this egret might extend a wing over an open pool to trick fish into swimming toward the shade. Once its prey is within range, the Snowy Egret plucks it from the false haven with the accuracy characteristic of all herons.

Like their kin, Snowy Egrets are social nesters. Their colonies consist of many shallow, stick platform nests placed low in trees or shrubs, usually interspersed with the nests of other herons. Nesting colonies are typically found on islands throughout Boston Harbor, and they are vulnerable to human disturbance. Visitors hoping to view these colonies should keep a respectful distance to ensure that the birds are not disturbed.

Similar Species: Great Egret is larger and has black feet. Black-crowned Night-Heron has a black cap and back, a gray neck and gray wings. Cattle Egret has a yellow bill and is smaller.

breeding

Jan Feb Mar Apr May Jun Jul Aug Sept Oct Nov Dec

Quick I.D.: mid-sized heron; sexes similar; all-white plumage; black bill and legs; yellow feet; yellow lore.
Size: 23 in.

Green Heron
Butorides virescens

This crow-sized heron is far less conspicuous than its Great Blue cousin. The Green Heron prefers to hunt for frogs and small fish in shallow, weedy wetlands, where it is often seen perched just above the water's surface. By searching the shallow, shady, overgrown, marshy edges of inland ponds and coastal shorelines, Boston birders can sometimes get a prolonged view of this otherwise reclusive bird.

The Green Heron often uses all of its stature to hunt over a favorite site. With its bright yellow or orange feet clasping a branch or reed, this small heron stretches nearly horizontally over the water, its pose rigid and unchanging until a fish swims into range. Like a taut bowstring, the tension mounts until the heron chooses to fire. Lunging its entire body at its prey, the heron is often soaked to the shoulders.

Similar Species: American Bittern is larger, is heavily streaked and lacks any green color. Virginia Rail (p. 23) lacks the green back and chestnut neck. Great Blue Heron (p. 20) is gray-blue and is twice as tall.

Quick I.D.: stubby, crow-sized heron; sexes similar; short legs; glossy green back; chestnut neck; dark cap.
Breeding male: orange legs. *Immature:* less colorful, with more streaking.
Size: 18–21 in.

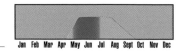

Virginia Rail
Rallus limicola

To best experience a Virginia Rail, sit patiently alongside a marsh. The slim bird may reveal itself for an instant to a determined observer, but most often the bird's voice is all that betrays its presence. Telegraph-like ticks and a descending *wak-wak-wak-wak-wak* call are normally the only evidence of breeding Virginia Rails. If you are lucky, a late-April visit to the marshes adjacent to East Squantum Street during high tide could be rewarded with the sounds or sightings of a Virginia Rail foraging along the marsh edge.

Virginia Rails build their raised nests in dense vegetation, using cattails, bulrushes and sedges. They often add a roof and a 'runway' to the nest if there is sufficient cover to hide the structure. Virginia Rails seldom leave their nesting marshes until winter ice forces them south, and they are infrequently seen flying, even though they are excellent long-distance migrants. When pursued by an intruder or predator, rails choose to scurry away through the dense, protective vegetation, rather than risk a getaway flight.

Similar Species: Sora has a black mask, a dark body and a short bill. Common Snipe has a longer bill, is heavily streaked and lacks the chestnut wing patch.

Jan Feb Mar Apr May Jun Jul Aug Sept Oct Nov Dec

Quick I.D.: robin-sized; sexes similar; cinnamon breast; large feet; long, reddish bill.
Size: 9–10½ in.

American Coot

Fulica americana

The American Coot is a curious mix of comedy and confusion: it seems to have been made up of bits and pieces leftover from other birds. It has the lobed toes of a grebe, the bill of a chicken and the body shape and swimming habits of a duck, but it is not remotely related to any of these species—its closest cousins are rails and cranes. American Coots dabble and dive in water and forage on land, and they eat both plant and animal matter. They can be found in many of the fresh- and saltwater marshes in the Boston area from September to April.

These loud, grouchy birds are usually seen chugging along in wetlands, frequently entering into short-lived disputes with other coots. American Coots appear comical when they swim: their heads bob in time with their paddling feet, and as a coot's swimming speed increases, so does the back-and-forth motion of its head. At peak speed, this motion seems to disorient the coot, so it prefers to run, flap and splash to the other side of the wetland.

Similar Species: All ducks and grebes generally lack the uniform black color and the all-white bill. Pied-billed Grebe is brown.

Quick I.D.: smaller than a duck; sexes similar; black body; white bill; red forehead shield; short tail; long legs; lobed feet; white undertail coverts.
Size: 14–16 in.

Jan Feb Mar Apr May Jun Jul Aug Sept Oct Nov Dec

Mute Swan
Cygnus olor

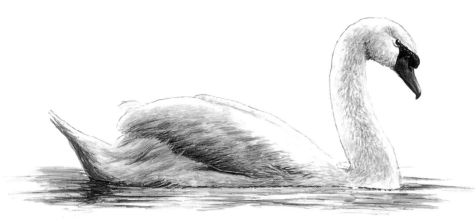

Gracing the waters of coastal Massachusetts, the Mute Swan looks and acts like a movie star. Its beautiful, silken wing plumes, the warm accents of black and orange on its head, and its romantic composure grant this bird a regal stature. The Mute Swan has a very nasty side, however, and it pinches and pecks at any individual, be it bird or human, that dares to challenge its space.

This Eurasian native, which was introduced to estate ponds and city parks throughout the eastern United States at the turn of the century, was considered to be a rare vagrant in Massachusetts as recently as 1955. A non-migrant, the Mute Swan appears to be a thriving summer breeder and winter resident in sheltered coastal waters to the north and south of Boston. As with so many introduced animals, the Mute Swan's population is expanding, and in some cases the Mute Swan is displacing native Massachusetts species and over-grazing vegetation locally.

Similar Species: Tundra Swan has an all-black bill that lacks a knob, and it holds its neck straighter.

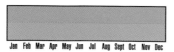

Jan Feb Mar Apr May Jun Jul Aug Sept Oct Nov Dec

Quick I.D.: larger than a goose; sexes similar; often swims with wings slightly raised; thick neck; black feet. *Adult:* all-white body; orange or pink bill with black knob at base. *Immature:* grayish-brownish body; all-dark bill.
Size: 52–60 in. (male slightly larger).

Canada Goose

Branta canadensis

Most flocks of Canada Geese in city parks and golf courses show little concern for their human neighbors. These urban geese seem to think nothing of creating a traffic jam, blocking a fairway or dining on a lawn. Their love of manicured parks and gardens and the lack of predators have created somewhat of a population explosion in many parts of the Boston area.

Breeding pairs of Canada Geese are regal in appearance, and their loyalty is legendary—they mate for life, and it's common for a mate to stay at the side of a fallen partner. Canadas that are permanent residents may be displacing migratory Canadas, which breed in Canada and migrate through Boston to winter farther south.

Similar Species: Brant lacks the white cheek, has a black upper breast and has a faint white 'necklace' across the front of the throat.

Quick I.D.: large goose; sexes similar; white cheek; black head and neck; brown body; white undertail coverts.
Size: 35–42 in.

Jan Feb Mar Apr May Jun Jul Aug Sept Oct Nov Dec

American Wigeon
Anas americana

During their spring and fall migrations, American Wigeons can easily be found and identified on freshwater ponds, including Fresh Pond. The white top and gray sides of the male American Wigeon's head look somewhat like a balding scalp, while the nasal *wee-he-he-he!* calls sound remarkably like the squeaks of a squeezed rubber ducky.

The concentrated spring run north is generally less productive for birdwatchers than the return of the birds through the month of October, when hundreds of wigeons can be seen on the water, feeding and refueling for the continuation of their southward trip. American Wigeons prefer to nest north of Massachusetts and tend to winter on sheltered ponds at Great Meadows and Parker River national wildlife refuges.

Similar Species: Green-winged Teal (p. 31) is smaller, has a white shoulder slash and has a rusty head with a green swipe. Eurasian Wigeon has a reddish head, gray back and gray sides.

Jan Feb Mar Apr May Jun Jul Aug Sept Oct Nov Dec

Quick I.D.: mid-sized duck; cinnamon breast and flanks; white belly; gray, black-tipped bill; green speculum. *Male:* white forehead; green swipe running back from eye. *Female:* no distinct colors on head. **Size:** 18–21 in.

American Black Duck

Anas rubripes

Among the flocks of waterfowl wintering on open water in the Boston area, you will find the plain-looking American Black Duck. Like a dark version of the familiar Mallard (except for its silver wing linings, dark orange feet and purple wing patch), the American Black Duck is the classic duck of eastern North America, and a healthy population resides in the Greater Boston area. American Black Ducks are more common on salt or brackish water; Mallards are more common on fresh water.

Unfortunately, the eastern expansion of Mallards has come at the expense of this dark dabbler. As its green-headed cousin spread into our area, the American Black Duck quickly hybridized with the Mallard. Some biologists are concerned about this genetic watering down of pure American Black Duck stock, and the future stability of the species is unknown. Habitat loss and the degradation of wetlands in general have further contributed to the decline of this bird. Although plain in appearance, the state of the Black Duck's future increases the profile of this East Coast specialty in the eyes and minds of conservation-oriented naturalists.

Similar Species: Mallard (p. 29) has an overall lighter body plumage and a blue speculum, and the male has a green head.

Quick I.D.: large duck; dark blackish-brown body; light brown head and neck; bright orange feet. *Male:* yellow bill. *Female:* dull green bill spotted with black. *In flight:* silver-lined wings.
Size: 22–24 in.

Jan Feb Mar Apr May Jun Jul Aug Sept Oct Nov Dec

Mallard
Anas platyrhynchos

The Mallard is the classic duck of inland marshes— the male's iridescent green head and chestnut breast are symbolic of wetland habitat. This large duck is commonly seen feeding in city parks and local ponds. It occasionally uses estuaries and protected coastal bays during the winter months. With their legs positioned under the middle part of their bodies, Mallards walk easily, and they can spring straight out of water without a running start.

Mallards are the most common duck in North America (and the Northern Hemisphere), and they are easily seen in Boston year-round. During winter, Mallards are seen in flocks of ducks on open water or grazing along shorelines. Because several duck species often band together in these loose flocks, birdwatchers habitually scan these groups to test their identification skills. Mallards (like all ducks) molt several times a year, so remember that the distinctive green head of the male Mallard occasionally loses its green pizzazz.

Similar Species: Female resembles many other female dabbling ducks, but look for the blue speculum, bordered by white on both sides, and her close association with the distinctive male. Male Northern Shoveler has a green head, a white breast, chestnut flanks and a much longer bill.

Quick I.D.: large duck; bright orange feet; blue speculum bordered by white.
Male: iridescent green head; bright yellow bill; chestnut breast; white flanks.
Female: mottled brown overall; bright orange bill marked with black.
Size: 22–26 in.

Jan Feb Mar Apr May Jun Jul Aug Sept Oct Nov Dec

Northern Pintail

Anas acuta

The Northern Pintail is often regarded as the most elegant duck to visit the Greater Boston area. The male's long tapering tail feathers and graceful neck contribute to the sleek appearance of this handsome bird. As winter frosts bear down upon northern lands, Northern Pintails are driven through the Boston area to escape the freeze-up. From late September through to the end of November, pintails descend from the cool autumn skies to fuel-up on aquatic plants and cultivated grains. During this time of year, pintails are encountered on lakes, saltwater bays, estuaries and tidal channels, characteristically 'tipping up' and extending their graceful tails skyward.

After spending their winter in warmer southern climes, Northern Pintails once again return to Boston's waters for March and April, moving north with warming spring breezes. Pair bonding, which begins on the wintering grounds, continues during migration, allowing newly formed pairs to begin their annual breeding ritual immediately upon arrival in suitable nesting habitat.

Similar Species: Mallard (p. 29), American Wigeon (p. 27) and Gadwall are all chunkier and lack the tapered tail.

Quick I.D.: large duck; long, slender neck; long, tapered tail; bluish bill. *In flight:* appears slender and sleek. *Male:* chocolate brown head; very long tail; white breast extending up base of neck; dusty gray body.
Female: mottled light brown overall.
Size: *Male:* 26–30 in. *Female:* 21–23 in.

Jan Feb Mar Apr May Jun Jul Aug Sept Oct Nov Dec

Green-winged Teal
Anas crecca

Like the Northern Pintail, the Green-winged Teal tends to only briefly visit the Boston area, always seeming to be on its way to some other place. Although this duck breeds in Massachusetts, Boston does not provide the concealing wetlands and densely vegetated pond habitats it needs to produce and raise its young successfully.

From mid-March to the end of April, and from early October to the end of November, this smallest North American dabbler is most often seen along the edges of ponds, estuaries and tidal marshes, such as those of Fresh Pond, Horn Pond, Mystic Lakes and Belle Isle Marsh. These small ducks prefer calm waters, where they often shun the company of larger waterfowl and remain with their own kind. When Green-winged Teals take to the air, they are among the fastest of ducks, showing their green inner wing patches amid a blur of wingbeats.

Similar Species: Blue-winged Teal has a blue wing patch and lacks the white undertail coverts, and the male has a steel blue head and a white crescent on the face. American Wigeon (p. 27) has a white forehead and a gray face. Eurasian Wigeon has a creamy forehead and lacks the green swipe.

Jan Feb Mar Apr May Jun Jul Aug Sept Oct Nov Dec

Quick I.D.: small duck; green wing patch. *Male:* chestnut head; green swipe trailing from eye; white, vertical shoulder slash; gray body. *Female:* mottled brown overall. **Size:** 14–16 in.

Canvasback

Aythya valisineria

During winter, hundreds of these white-backed ducks can often be seen on Fresh Pond and other similar inland waterbodies, majestically swimming in open waters with their bills held high. Canvasbacks are deepwater ducks, and they acquire their vegetarian diet in well-spaced dives. Birders can easily identify the stately Canvasback at a distance. Its distinctive profile results from the apparent lack of a forehead—the dark bill appears to run straight up to the top of the bird's head, giving the Canvasback sleek, hydrodynamic-looking contours.

The Redhead is a closely related duck that is very similar in appearance. Like the male Canvasback's, the male Redhead's head is—you guessed it—red, but its back is gray instead of white. Also, the Redhead has a noticeable forehead, just like it is wearing a ball cap.

Similar Species: Greater Scaup (p. 34) and Lesser Scaup lack the chestnut head and the sloping forehead. Redhead lacks the sloping forehead and has a black-tipped, gray bill and a darker back.

Quick I.D.: large duck; sloping, black bill and forehead. *Male:* canvas white back; chestnut head; black breast and hindquarters. *Female:* brown head and neck; lighter body.
Size: 19–22 in.

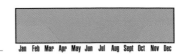

Jan Feb Mar Apr May Jun Jul Aug Sept Oct Nov Dec

Ring-necked Duck
Aythya collaris

Another of our brief, migratory visitors, the Ring-necked Duck is often seen among Canvasbacks on Fresh Pond in March and November. These diving ducks prefer ponds and lakes with muddy bottoms. They dive deeply underwater for aquatic invertebrates and aquatic vegetation, including seeds, tubers and pondweed leaves. Because of their foraging habits, Ring-necked Ducks are susceptible to ingesting poisonous lead shot—wasted shotgun pellets lie at the bottom of many rural wetlands throughout this duck's summer and winter range.

Although this duck's name implies the presence of a collar, most experienced birders have given up on seeing this faint feature. The only prominent ring noticeable in field observations is around the tip of the bill, suggesting that a more reasonable name for this bird would have been 'Ring-billed Duck.'

Similar Species: Greater Scaup (p. 34) and Lesser Scaup lack the white shoulder slash and the black back. Female Redhead has a dark brown head to match its body.

Quick I.D.: mid-sized duck; black bill tip; white bill ring. *Male:* dark head with hints of purple; black breast, back and hindquarters; white shoulder slash; gray sides.
Female: dark brown body; light brown head (lighter brown close to bill); white eye ring and eye line.
Size: 17 in.

Jan Feb Mar Apr May Jun Jul Aug Sept Oct Nov Dec

Greater Scaup
Aythya marila

The Greater Scaup is the Oreo cookie of the coastal ducks—black at both ends and white in the middle. It is a diving duck that prefers deep, open water, and, during winter, thousands of them can be seen plying the waters of Quincy Bay.

Most ducks seen in deep water are diving ducks, while those seen on shallow ponds or walking on land tend to be dabbling ducks. Diving ducks have smaller wings, which helps them underwater but makes for difficult take-offs and landings. When a duck scoots across the water in an attempt to get airborne, even a first-time birder can tell it's a diver. Divers' legs are placed well back on their bodies—an advantage for underwater swimming, but not for easy walking. All ducks are front-heavy, so in order for diving ducks to stand, they must raise their front ends high to maintain balance.

Similar Species: Lesser Scaup has a purplish tinge to its head and tends to occur in smaller flocks on fresh water. Ring-necked Duck (p. 33) has a black back and a white shoulder slash. Common Goldeneye has a white breast.

Quick I.D.: mid-sized duck. *Male:* dark, rounded head with hints of green; black breast and hindquarters; grayish-white sides and upperparts. *Female:* dark brown; well-defined white patch at base of bill.
Size: 18 in.

Common Eider
Somateria mollissima

Thousands of Common Eiders regularly float on the frigid winter waters of Massachusetts Bay, while leisurely waterproofing their feathers in preparation for the next dive. Look for them off Heath Park at the north end of Winthrop Beach. Like scoters, these hefty birds are well adapted for living among the frothy ocean waves of cold northern seas and for feeding on ocean mollusks. Swallowed whole, the mollusk is crushed into small fragments in the bird's gizzard, which lets the bird digest its meal more quickly, extracting the much-needed nutrients and heat-producing energy.

In addition to the waterproofing oil produced by the preen gland, eiders also get insulation from their soft, dense inner feathers, which trap warm air near the body. On their northern breeding grounds, colony-nesting females pluck these downy feathers from their own bodies to provide insulation and camouflage for their precious eggs. For centuries, people have prized eider down collected from nest sites as a superior form of natural insulation.

Similar Species: Male King Eider has a colorful, blocky head. Male scoters lack the white breast and back, and females lack the barring. Oldsquaw (p. 37), Bufflehead (p. 38) and Common Goldeneye all lack the smoothly sloping forehead.

Quick I.D.: large duck; smoothly sloping forehead. *Male:* black and white, with green tinge on nape and nasal shield. *Female:* rusty brown, with barred breast, flanks and back; gray bill and nasal shield.
Immature male: dark head and body with white breast. *In flight:* flies close to water surface with lowered head.
Size: 22–26 in.

Jan Feb Mar Apr May Jun Jul Aug Sept Oct Nov Dec

White-winged Scoter
Melanitta fusca

As White-winged Scoters race across choppy winter seas, their flapping wings reveal this bird's key diagnostic feature—the white inner wing patches strike a sharp contrast with the bird's otherwise all-black plumage and the dark waters.

Scoters are heavy-bodied ducks that use both their feet and their partially spread wings in deep foraging dives, which can last up to one minute or so. These large ducks form rafts on the offshore waters, where they dive for snails, mussels, clams and crustaceans. The gizzards of scoters are exceptionally strong, and they can grind these hard-shell invertebrates into digestible matter.

Black Scoters, the rarest of the three scoters, also occur in the Boston area. These all-black birds winter on Massachusetts Bay, and they are often seen in mixed-species rafts with White-winged Scoters and Surf Scoters.

Similar Species: Surf Scoter lacks the white wing patches, and the male has a white forehead and nape. Black Scoter is all black, with no white on its wings or head, and it has a bulbous, orange bill.

Quick I.D.: large, stocky duck; white wing patch; large bill; sloping forehead; base of bill is fully feathered. *Male:* black overall; white eye patch. *Female:* brown overall; gray-brown bill; light patches on cheek and ear.
Size: 20–23 in.

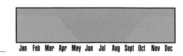

Jan Feb Mar Apr May Jun Jul Aug Sept Oct Nov Dec

Oldsquaw

Clangula hyemalis

Oldsquaws are tough ducks that visit Boston during the harshest time of year. It is the predominantly white winter plumage that is most frequently seen on our waters as Oldsquaws linger in the Boston area throughout the coldest months. The spring breeding plumage of these Arctic-nesting sea ducks—mostly dark with white highlights—is like a photo-negative of the winter plumage.

These handsome ducks typically sit in rafts a mile or more offshore, limiting observers to brief glimpses of their long, slender tail feathers. During their stay here, Oldsquaws can often be quite vocal, filling the coastal breeze with their distinctive cries. While foraging for minnows, crustaceans and mollusks, they calmly dive to the bottom of ocean bays for up to 30 seconds. Small numbers of Oldsquaws can usually be seen and heard off any harbor, but Fresh Pond and Nahant are also good places to look.

Similar Species: None.

winter

Quick I.D.: small duck; male has long tail feathers. *Winter male:* white head, flanks, back and underparts; dark cheek, breast and wings. *Winter female:* dark back; light underparts. *Summer male:* dark head, back and neck; white cheek and underparts; pink bill with black tip and base. *Summer female:* light flanks and head; dark cheek.
Size: 17–20 in.

Jan Feb Mar Apr May Jun Jul Aug Sept Oct Nov Dec

Bufflehead
Bucephala albeola

The small, 'baby-faced' Bufflehead is perhaps the cutest of Boston's ducks; its simple plumage and rotund physique bring to mind a child's stuffed toy. During the fall migration and winter, these charming birds are commonly seen on Fresh Pond, Lynn Harbor and Nahant Bay.

Because ducks spend most of their lives dripping with water, preening is an important behavior. At the base of the tail of most birds lies the preen (uropygial) gland, which secretes a viscous liquid that inhibits bacterial growth and waterproofs and conditions the feathers. After gently squeezing the preen gland with its bill, a bird can spread the secretion methodically over most of its body, an essential practice to revitalize precious feathers. Because sun, wind and salt water damage feathers, it is understandable that birds spend so much time in the preening and maintenance of their feathers.

Similar Species: Male Common Goldeneye is larger and lacks the white, unbordered triangle behind the eye.

Quick I.D.: tiny duck; round body.
Male: white triangle on back of otherwise dark head; white body; dark back.
Female: dirty brown; small white cheek patch.
Size: 13–15 in.

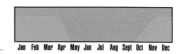

Jan Feb Mar Apr May Jun Jul Aug Sept Oct Nov Dec

Red-breasted Merganser

Mergus serrator

The productive, sheltered waters of the Boston coastline provide excellent wintering habitat for the Red-breasted Merganser. Unlike the Common Merganser, which spends winter on inland lakes, ponds and streams, the Red-breasted Merganser retreats to rich coastal habitats to endure the chills of winter. This sleek diving duck uses its powerful legs to propel itself underwater in pursuit of fish. Small groups of these mergansers can often be seen fishing co-operatively, encircling and trapping small schools of fish.

As warm spring weather arrives in the Boston area, Red-breasted Mergansers congregate along the coast in larger numbers. At this time of year, the males, with their reddish breasts and punk hairdos, initiate their courting rituals before their final push north to inland, freshwater breeding grounds. As small V-shaped flocks fly past Belle Isle and World's End, look for the flashing, white inner wing patches that characterize this species.

Similar Species: Male Common Merganser lacks the red breast and has white underparts, and the female has a well-defined, reddish-brown hood. Common Loon (p. 16) and other large ducks lack the combination of a green head, an orange bill, orange feet and a red breast.

Quick I.D.: large duck; gray body.
Male: well-defined, dark green hood; punk-like crest; streaked, red breast; white collar; brilliant orange bill and feet; black spinal streak. *Female:* rusty hood blending into white breast.
Size: 21–25 in.

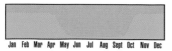

Jan Feb Mar Apr May Jun Jul Aug Sept Oct Nov Dec

Ruddy Duck

Oxyura jamaicensis

On their northern breeding grounds, male Ruddy Ducks are known as the clowns of freshwater wetlands for their comical courtship antics and colorful breeding attire (including a bright blue bill). Unfortunately, Bostonians rarely see this side of Ruddy Duck life; we are usually limited to observing these stiff-tailed diving ducks during their brief fall migration.

During fall and over winter, these ducks spend much of their time diving for food. At the bottom of freshwater ponds and estuaries they use their broad bills to strain seeds, roots, other vegetation and aquatic invertebrates from the soft, muddy substrate. Ruddy Ducks rarely associate with other species of waterfowl, but they can occasionally be seen mingling among American Coots. When approached by danger, these ducks prefer to dive rather than take flight. This habit, in combination with the tendency of 'Ruddies' to migrate at night, means that few birders will get a chance to observe this bird in flight.

Similar Species: Female Bufflehead (p. 38) has a white cheek patch, like a winter male Ruddy Duck. All other waterfowl are generally larger and have shorter tails and relatively smaller heads.

non-breeding

Quick I.D.: small duck; broad bill; large head; tail is often cocked up. *Breeding male:* reddish-brown neck and body; black head and tail; white cheek; blue bill. *Non-breeding male:* dull brown overall; dark cap; white cheek. *Female:* like non-breeding male, but pale cheek has a dark stripe.
Size: 14–16 in.

Jan Feb Mar Apr May Jun Jul Aug Sept Oct Nov Dec

Turkey Vulture
Cathartes aura

Soaring effortlessly above the Blue Hills Reservation, Turkey Vultures ride rising thermals on warm summer afternoons. They seldom need to flap their silver-lined wings, and they rock gently from side to side as they carefully scan fields, roads, woodlands and shorelines for carcasses. Even at great distances, this bare-headed bird can be identified by the way it tends to hold its wings upward in a shallow V.

The Turkey Vulture feeds entirely on carrion, which it can sometimes detect by scent alone. Its head is featherless, which is an adaptation to staying clean and parasite-free while it digs around inside carcasses. This scavenger's well-known habit of regurgitating its rotting meal at intruders might be a defense mechanism—it allows Turkey Vultures to reduce their weight for a quicker take-off, and the smell helps young vultures repel would-be predators.

Similar Species: Hawks, eagles and Osprey (p. 43) all have large, feathered heads and tend to hold their wings flatter in flight, not in a shallow V.

Quick I.D.: larger than a hawk; sexes similar; all black; small, red head.
In flight: wings held in shallow V; silver-gray flight feathers; dark wing linings; rocks from side to side.
Size: 27–30 in.

Jan Feb Mar Apr May Jun Jul Aug Sept Oct Nov Dec

Bald Eagle
Haliaeetus leucocephalus

Bald Eagles are adept at catching fish, which they pluck from just below the water's surface. These easy-living eagles spend much of their lives perched high in trees overlooking inland lakes, rivers and coastal bays. The dignified appearance of America's national emblem masks their unsavory habit of scavenging prey and pirating fish from Osprey.

Like many other raptors, Bald Eagles had virtually disappeared from Massachusetts by the 1960s. Fortunately, the banning of DDT and efforts to re-establish nesting pairs at Quabbin Reservoir have resulted in stronger eagle populations. Although they are still uncommon, more and more eagles can be seen soaring over the Boston area, particularly during winter and in migration.

A Bald Eagle takes four or five years to acquire its distinctive white tail and head, but younger birds are easily distinguished by their 6½-foot wingspan. No one can help but appreciate the sight of a mature eagle spotted within sight of down-town Boston.

Similar Species: Osprey (p. 43) is smaller and has a black stripe through its white head. Turkey Vulture (p. 41) has a small, naked, red head and silver flight feathers, and its wings are often held in a shallow V.

Quick I.D.: much larger than a hawk; sexes similar. *Adult:* unmistakable white head and tail; dark brown body and wings; yellow bill and talons. *Immature* (1–5 years old): variable in plumage, but always large in size; mostly dark brown; certain plumages are heavily blotched in white.
Size: 35–40 in.

Jan Feb Mar Apr May Jun Jul Aug Sept Oct Nov Dec

Osprey
Pandion haliaetus

In the Boston area, the Osprey is most often seen over large waterbodies during its migration, which extends from mid-April to early May in spring and throughout September in fall. Although a large population of Ospreys nests southeast of Boston around Cape Cod and Nantucket, only recently have these birds begun to reclaim their breeding range closer to Boston.

A hunting Osprey will survey the calm waters of a coastal bay from the air. Spotting a flash of silver at the water's surface, the Osprey folds its great wings and dives toward the fish. An instant before striking the water, the bird thrusts its talons forward to grasp its slippery prey. The Osprey might completely disappear beneath the water to ensure a successful capture; then it reappears, slapping its wings on the surface as it returns to the air. Once it has regained flight, the Osprey shakes off the residual water and heads off toward its bulky stick nest, holding its prey facing forward to increase aerodynamic efficiency.

Similar Species: Bald Eagle (p. 42) is larger and never has the combination of white underparts and a white head with an eye streak. Other large raptors are seldom seen near water. Gulls are smaller and have more pointed wings.

Jan Feb Mar Apr May Jun Jul Aug Sept Oct Nov Dec

Quick I.D.: large hawk–sized; sexes similar; white underparts; dark elbow patches; white head; dark streak through eye.
In flight: wings held in shallow M.
Size: 21–24 in.

Northern Harrier

Circus cyaneus

♀

This common marsh hawk can best be identified by its flight behavior: the Northern Harrier flies low over lush meadows, often retracing its path several times in the quest for prey. Watch the slow, lazy wingbeats of the Northern Harrier as this raptor skims the brambles and bulrushes with its belly. Unlike other hawks, which can find their prey only visually, the Northern Harrier stays close enough to the ground to listen for birds, voles and mice. When movement catches the harrier's eyes or ears, it abandons its lazy ways to strike at prey with channeled energy.

Hunting harriers are best found during April and October as they migrate along the coast. They are most often observed over salt marshes, grassy expanses and the shorelines of estuaries, like those found at Belle Isle and Logan Airport.

Similar Species: Short-eared Owl and Sharp-shinned (p. 45), Red-tailed (p. 47) and Cooper's hawks all lack the white rump. Rough-legged Hawk has a white rump, but it has a chunkier shape (shorter, broader wings and tail).

Quick I.D.: mid-sized hawk; white rump; long tail; long wings; owl-like face (seen only at close range). *Male:* grayish upperparts; whitish underparts; black wing tips. *Female:* brown overall. *Immature:* chestnut overall. **Size:** 20 in.

Jan Feb Mar Apr May Jun Jul Aug Sept Oct Nov Dec

Sharp-shinned Hawk
Accipiter striatus

If songbirds dream, the Sharp-shinned Hawk is sure to be the source of their nightmares. These raptors pursue small birds through forests, maneuvering around leaves and branches in the hope of striking down prey. Sharp-shinned Hawks prey on many birds, with small songbirds and the occasional woodpecker being the most numerous prey items.

These small hawks are easy to find in wooded areas and in open skies as they pass through our area in April and again in late September. During the winter months, at least a few of Boston's wooded neighborhoods have a resident 'Sharpie' eager to catch unwary finches, sparrows and starlings. Backyard feeders tend to concentrate sparrows and finches, so they are attractive foraging areas for this small hawk. A sudden eruption of songbirds off the feeder and a few feathers floating on the wind are often the signs of a sudden, successful Sharp-shin attack.

Similar Species: Cooper's Hawk is larger, and its tail is rounded and has a wide terminal band. Merlin has pointed wings and rapid wingbeats, and it lacks the red breast barring of an adult Sharp-shinned Hawk.

Quick I.D.: pigeon-sized; sexes similar; short, round wings; long tail. *Adult:* blue-gray back; red barring on underparts; red eyes. *Immature:* brown overall; vertical, brown streaks on breast; yellow eyes. *In flight:* flap-and-glide flier; barred tail is straight at end. **Size:** 12–14 in. (female larger).

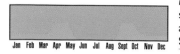

Jan Feb Mar Apr May Jun Jul Aug Sept Oct Nov Dec

Broad-winged Hawk

Buteo platypterus

Sighting this mid-sized hawk is a hit-and-miss affair. Broad-winged Hawks are fairly secretive in their wooded breeding habitat, and many summers can pass without one being seen, even though they regularly breed in the wooded areas of Greater Boston. A trip to Mt. Tom or Mt. Wachusett on April 20 to 30 or September 12 to 20 can be a spectacular experience, however, because tens of thousands of migrating Broad-winged Hawks can often be seen in a single day! This peak of migration might occur on only three or four days, and the fall flights are best when driven by northeasterly winds.

Hawks' heavy wings are not designed for continual flapping flight, so these raptors seek out areas such as hills and mountains where they can soar on warm updrafts. The rising air currents help them gain altitude before they launch across a stretch of stagnant, heavy air.

Similar Species: Red-tailed Hawk (p. 47) has a solid red tail. Sharp-shinned Hawk (p. 45) has a long, narrow tail. Rough-legged Hawk is a winter visitor. Red-shouldered Hawk has red shoulders and narrow, white bands on its black tail.

Quick I.D.: smaller than a crow; sexes similar; wide, white bands on black, fan-like tail; russet barring on breast; rounded wings.
Size: 15–17 in.

Jan Feb Mar Apr May Jun Jul Aug Sept Oct Nov Dec

Red-tailed Hawk

Buteo jamaicensis

With its fierce facial expression and untidy feathers, the Red-tailed Hawk looks as though it has been suddenly and rudely awakened. Its characteristic scream further suggests that the Red-tailed Hawk is a bird best avoided. You would think other birds would treat this large raptor with more respect, but the Red-tailed Hawk is constantly being harassed by crows, jays and blackbirds.

It isn't until this hawk is two or three years old that its tail becomes brick red. The dark head, the dark 'belt' around its midsection and the dark leading edge to its wings are better field marks, because they're seen in most Red-tails. Wherever highways pass through open country, it's hard not to spot a Red-tail perched on a post or soaring lazily overhead.

Similar Species: Northern Harrier (p. 44) has a white rump and a long tail. Sharp-shinned Hawk (p. 45) and Cooper's Hawk are smaller and have long, slender tails. Broad-winged Hawk (p. 46) has a boldly banded tail.

Jan Feb Mar Apr May Jun Jul Aug Sept Oct Nov Dec

Quick I.D.: large hawk; sexes similar; brick red tail (adult only); brown head; variable, brown-speckled 'belt'; light flight feathers; dark wing lining and leading edge.
Size: 20–24 in.

VULTURES, HAWKS & FALCONS 47

American Kestrel

Falco sparverius

This small, noisy falcon is a common summer sight over much of the Boston area. It has adapted well to urban life, and it is commonly seen perched on power lines, watching for unwary grasshoppers, birds and rodents. When not perched, American Kestrels can often be seen hovering above potential prey. All falcons are skilled hunters, and they have a unique, tooth-like projection on their hooked bills that can quickly crush the necks of small prey. The American Kestrel's species name, *sparverius*, is Latin for 'pertaining to sparrows,' which are occasional prey items.

American Kestrels often build their nests in abandoned woodpecker cavities. Conservationists have recently discovered that kestrels will use nest boxes when natural cavities are unavailable, which should ensure that these active predators remain common throughout the Boston area.

Similar Species: Sharp-shinned Hawk (p. 45) and Cooper's Hawk have short, rounder wings. Merlin is larger, has a banded tail and has boldly streaked underparts.

Quick I.D.: smaller than a jay; long, pointed wings; long tail; two vertical, black stripes on each side of face; spotted breast; hooked bill. *In flight:* rapid wingbeat. *Male:* blue wings; russet back; colorful head. *Female:* russet back and wings.
Size: 9–11 in.

Jan Feb Mar Apr May Jun Jul Aug Sept Oct Nov Dec

Northern Bobwhite

Colinus virginianus

As the East's only native quail, the Northern Bobwhite alone displays this group's unusual behaviors to Boston-area naturalists. In early spring, a rising, whistled *bob-white!* call often bursts from a dense brush pile or hedgerow. Although their calls give away the bobwhites' identity, the scurrying birds often refuse to be seen—they stubbornly remain hidden in protective cover.

Outside the brief spring courtship season, Northern Bobwhites gather in groups of typically about a dozen birds. Known as 'coveys,' these marauding bands forage widely for seeds, leaves and insects on farmlands and along habitat edges in our area. Boston is near the northern limit of this quail's natural range, and our winters can be quite hard on these small birds. Coveys roost together on the ground in circles, with the birds' tails pointing inward and their heads pointing out. This unusual behavior is not only effective in sharing communal warmth, it also ensures that each bird has a clear take-off path should a threat arise.

Similar Species: None.

Quick I.D.: larger than a robin; plump, reddish-brown body; short tail; chestnut streaks on flanks. *Male:* bold, black-and-white facial pattern; white throat. *Female:* black-and-buff facial pattern; buff throat. **Size:** 10 in.

Jan Feb Mar Apr May Jun Jul Aug Sept Oct Nov Dec

Black-bellied Plover
Pluvialis squatarola

During winter, Black-bellied Plovers are rarely seen darting along sea beaches, grassy openings and plowed fields, foraging with a robin-like run-and-stop technique. Although they dress in plain grays for much of their Boston retreat, many Black-bellied Plovers can be seen in their summer 'tuxedo' plumage in late spring and early fall.

Although these plovers are most common in the Boston area during their spring and fall migrations, a few birds can usually be observed poking around our beaches in summer and winter. Bring your binoculars with you on your next walk along Revere Beach or Winthrop Beach—if you're lucky, you might see some Black-bellied Plovers scurrying along the sand as they pluck the surface for food.

Similar Species: Red Knot (p. 58) in winter plumage looks very similar. Willet is larger and slimmer and has a longer bill. Other shorebirds don't use the run-and-stop feeding technique and are not as plump or as gray.

non-breeding

Quick I.D.: larger than a robin; sexes similar; short, stout, black bill; relatively long, dark legs. *Breeding:* black and white. *Non-breeding:* slightly streaked, gray body. *In flight:* black wing pits; white rump; white wing linings.
Size: 12 in.

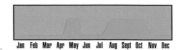

Jan Feb Mar Apr May Jun Jul Aug Sept Oct Nov Dec

Piping Plover
Charadrius melodus

breeding

♂

A master of illusion, the secretive Piping Plover is a rarely seen bird of the sandy ocean shore. Its pale body colors conceal it among the shoreline sand, while the dark bands across the forehead and breast look like stray pebbles or strips of washed-up vegetation that effectively disrupt its body form so that it no longer looks like a bird to potential predators. Even its four pale, pear-shaped eggs are speckled with dark colors to disguise them among the combination of sand, rocks, vegetation and scattered shell fragments that surround a typical nest.

Unfortunately, increased competition with people seeking the use of the beautiful shoreline landscape continues to threaten the breeding success of this delightful but increasingly endangered bird. Learning to recognize its presence along the beaches of Massachusetts Bay and helping to promote its needs for privacy might ensure that it remains a treasured part of Boston for years to come.

Similar Species: Semipalmated Plover has dark back and dark facial bands connecting the eyes to the bill.

Quick I.D.: smaller than a robin; sexes similar; white underside; pale gray back; black forehead band connecting eyes; black collar band often connects across breast; white rump in flight; orange legs; orange bill tipped with black.
Size: 7¼ in.

Jan Feb Mar Apr May Jun Jul Aug Sept Oct Nov Dec

Killdeer

Charadrius vociferus

The Killdeer is the most widespread shorebird in the Boston area. It nests on gravelly shorelines, utility rights-of-way, lawns, pastures and occasionally on gravel roofs and parking lots within cities. Its name is a paraphrase of its distinctive, loud call: *kill-dee kill-dee kill-deer!*

The Killdeer's response to predators relies on deception and good acting skills. To divert a predator's attention away from a nest or a brood of young, an adult Killdeer (like many shorebirds) will flop around to feign an injury (usually a broken wing). Once the Killdeer has the attention of the fox, crow, gull or human, it leads the predator away from the vulnerable nest. After it reaches a safe distance, the adult Killdeer is suddenly 'healed' and flies off, leaving the predator without a meal.

Similar Species: Semipalmated Plover has only one breast band, is smaller and is found mostly on mudflats.

Quick I.D.: robin-sized; sexes similar; two black bands across breast; brown back; russet rump; long legs; white underparts.
Size: 9–11 in.

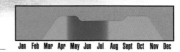

Jan Feb Mar Apr May Jun Jul Aug Sept Oct Nov Dec

American Oystercatcher
Haematopus palliatus

Wouldn't life be great if you could just leave the city rat-race behind to spend every day wading in the ocean surf, eating fresh, tasty seafood morsels and catching some of those precious rays of Atlantic coast sunshine? And, of course, there is nothing like rounding out each day with some 'wing-surfing' on the salty ocean breeze. If only we were as lucky as those peculiar American Oystercatchers!

These large, stocky shorebirds with long, razor-sharp bills specialize in prying or hammering open oysters, clams, mussels and other shellfish. When their taste buds cry out for more, however, and when the opportunity arises, they will gladly eat a whole host of other intertidal invertebrates, including limpets, crabs, marine worms, sea urchins, chitons and even jellyfish. During the summer breeding season, watch for mating pairs of these unmistakable birds performing their loud 'piping' courtship display around Boston Harbor.

Similar Species: Willet has the black-and-white wing pattern, but it has gray body plumage and lacks the thick, orange-red bill.

Jan Feb Mar Apr May Jun Jul Aug Sept Oct Nov Dec

Quick I.D.: gull-sized; sexes similar; long orange-red bill; black head and neck; brown back; white wing and rump patches; white underparts.
Size: 18½ in.

Greater Yellowlegs

Tringa melanoleuca

On a spring walk along the shores of Massachusetts Bay, you can see quite a few different sandpipers. The Greater Yellowlegs prefers shallow pools where it can peck for small invertebrates, but it won't hestitate to also venture belly-deep into the water to pursue prey. Occasionally, a yellowlegs can be seen hopping along on one leg, with the other one tucked up in the body feathers to reduce heat loss.

Many birders enjoy the challenge of distinguishing the Greater Yellowlegs from the Lesser Yellowlegs. The Greater, which is slightly more common in the Boston area (but don't let that bias your identification), has a relatively longer, heavier bill. The Greater's bill is also slightly upturned—so slightly, however, that you notice it one moment and not the next. Generally, the Lesser's call is *tew tew*, and the Greater's is *tew tew tew*. Cocky birders will name them at a glance, but more experienced birders will tell you that many of these people are bluffing—much of the time you can only write 'unidentified yellowlegs' in your field notes.

Similar Species: Lesser Yellowlegs is smaller and has a shorter bill. Western Sandpiper, Sanderling (p. 59) and Dunlin (p. 63) are all much smaller and have dark legs. Willet has bluish legs and a shorter, straighter bill.

non-breeding

Quick I.D.: pigeon-sized; sexes similar; long, bright yellow legs; finely streaked, gray body; bill is longer than head width.
Size: 13–15 in.

Jan Feb Mar Apr May Jun Jul Aug Sept Oct Nov Dec

Spotted Sandpiper
Actitis macularia

breeding

This common shorebird of lakes, rivers and coastlines has a most uncommon mating strategy. In a reversal of the gender roles of most birds, female Spotted Sandpipers compete for the males in spring. After the nest is built and the eggs are laid, the female leaves to find another mate, while the first male incubates the eggs. This behavior can be repeated two or more times before the female settles down with one male to raise her last brood of chicks.

The Spotted Sandpiper is readily identified by its arthritic-looking, stiff-winged flights low over the water. Its peppy call—*eat-wheat wheat-wheat-wheat*—bursts from startled birds as they retreat from shoreline disturbances. Spotted Sandpipers nest in the Boston area, and during the migratory months they are frequently encountered along undisturbed shores and rocky piers. They constantly teeter and bob when they are not in flight, which makes them easy to identify.

Similar Species: Killdeer (p. 52) has dark throat bands. Solitary Sandpiper has an eye ring and lacks the prominent breast spots. Lesser Yellowlegs has longer legs.

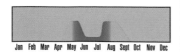

Jan Feb Mar Apr May Jun Jul Aug Sept Oct Nov Dec

Quick I.D.: smaller than a robin; often teeters and bobs; yellow legs.
Breeding: spotted breast (more pronounced in female); olive-gray back; yellow bill tipped with black.
Size: 7–8 in.

Hudsonian Godwit
Limosa haemastica

In a brief but dramatic appearance along our shorelines from late July to October, many of these large, leggy shorebirds make a quick, last minute pit-stop before flying non-stop over the Atlantic Ocean to northern South America. Hudsonian Godwits do not appear in the Boston area during their spring migration—they fly over the Great Plains on the northward journey to their arctic breeding grounds.

Like other long-billed shorebirds, the Hudsonian Godwit specializes in foraging for a variety of small invertebrates. While wading through the watery tide, this godwit inserts its long bill into the mud and sand of the bottom, quickly snatching up items it detects by feel. Some observers have reported seeing this bird wading through deep water up to its head! Point of Pines, Belle Isle Marsh and Newburyport are the best places to find these white-rumped birds, especially during the hours immediately before or after low tide.

Similar Species: Marbled Godwit lacks the white rump, the light flight feathers, the black wing pits and the black tail. Greater Yellowlegs (p. 54) has yellow legs and a much shorter, all-black bill. Short-billed Dowitcher (p. 64) has a barred tail, a white wedge on the lower back, greenish legs and a shorter, all-black bill.

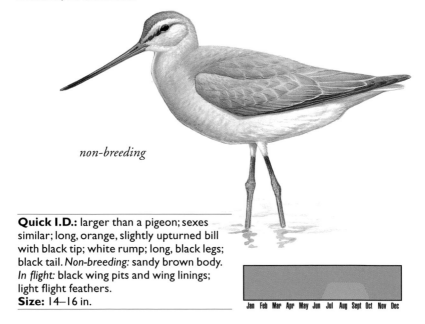

non-breeding

Quick I.D.: larger than a pigeon; sexes similar; long, orange, slightly upturned bill with black tip; white rump; long, black legs; black tail. *Non-breeding:* sandy brown body. *In flight:* black wing pits and wing linings; light flight feathers.
Size: 14–16 in.

Jan Feb Mar Apr May Jun Jul Aug Sept Oct Nov Dec

Ruddy Turnstone

Arenaria interpres

During migration, Ruddies prefer to stop on sandy and pebbly beaches, which are found in many areas around Boston. Ruddy Turnstones can often be seen on beaches at Nahant and Point Allerton and along the breakwaters of Winthrop Beach at high tide. They are often seen in good numbers mixed in with other species of shorebirds.

Ruddy Turnstones do much of their foraging by probing in the wet sand and between small rocks for amphipods, isopods and other small invertebrates that live buried along the shoreline, but they have gained fame for an unusual feeding technique. As its name implies, a turnstone often flips over small rocks and ocean debris with its bill to expose hidden invertebrates. The turnstone's bill is short, stubby and slightly upturned—ideal for this foraging style.

Similar Species: Dunlin (p. 63) has a downcurved bill and lacks the bold pattering.

non-breeding

Jan Feb Mar Apr May Jun Jul Aug Sept Oct Nov Dec

Quick I.D.: robin-sized; sexes similar (female is slightly paler); white belly; black bib; stout, slightly upturned bill; orange-red legs. *Breeding:* ruddy upperparts; white face; black collar; gray crown. *Non-breeding:* dark brownish upperparts and face.
Size: 9–10 in.

Red Knot

Calidris canutus

non-breeding

This shorebird favors invertebrate-rich mudflats and beaches at low tide. The Red Knot is commonly seen along Winthrop Beach and similar Boston-area shores during its spring and fall migrations, although birdwatchers out scanning the beaches in fall should be warned that at that time of year a Red Knot is not red. It often converges in flocks of thousands of birds that stop to refuel enroute between their arctic breeding grounds and southerly wintering grounds.

Carolus Linnaeus, the 'father' of modern scientific nomenclature, named the Red Knot *canutus* after King Canute, an 11th-century king of Denmark, England and Norway. According to some stories, the king had a great appreciation for these birds—as a main course for supper. Canute is sometimes called 'Knut,' which seems to be the source of the common name 'knot.'

Similar Species: Black-bellied Plover (p. 50) in winter plumage looks very similar. Long-billed Dowitcher, Short-billed Dowitcher (p. 64) and American Woodcock (p. 65) all have much longer bills (at least 1¹/₂ times longer than the width of their heads).

Quick I.D.: robin-sized; sexes similar; stout body; straight, black bill (slightly longer than head width). *Breeding:* rusty-orange face, neck, breast and flanks; mottled back (rust, brown and black). *Non-breeding:* grayish upperparts; white underparts; faint streaking on breast; white wing stripe; faint grayish barring on white rump.
Size: 10¹/₂ in.

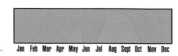

Jan Feb Mar Apr May Jun Jul Aug Sept Oct Nov Dec

Sanderling
Calidris alba

A spring or fall stroll at Revere or Winthrop beach is often punctuated by the sight of these tiny runners, which appear to enjoy nothing more than playing in the surf. Sanderlings are characteristically seen chasing and retreating from the rolling waves, never getting caught in the charging water. Only the Sanderling commonly forages in this manner, plucking at the exposed invertebrates stirred up by the wave action. When there are no waves to chase along calm shorelines, Sanderlings unenthusiastically probe into wet soil in much the same fashion as many other sandpipers.

This sandpiper is one of the world's most widespread birds. It breeds across the Arctic in Alaska, Canada and Russia, and it spends the winter running up and down sandy shorelines in North America, South America, Asia, Africa and Australia. Every year, a few hundred of these birds choose to brave winter along the wave-swept beaches of Massachusetts Bay.

Similar Species: Least Sandpiper (p. 61) is smaller and darker. Dunlin (p. 63) is darker and has a downcurved bill.

non-breeding

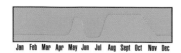

Jan Feb Mar Apr May Jun Jul Aug Sept Oct Nov Dec

Quick I.D.: smaller than a robin; sexes similar; straight, black bill; dark legs. *Breeding:* rusty head and breast. *Non-breeding:* white underparts; grayish-white upperparts; black shoulder patch (sometimes concealed). **Size:** 7¹/₂–8¹/₂ in.

Semipalmated Sandpiper
Calidris pusilla

Boston birders are privileged to feast twice each year on the great migrations of these spectacular 'wind birds.' In late May and again from late July to October, Boston-area shorelines are visited by synchronized flocks of Semipalmated Sandpipers. They peck and probe in mechanized fury, replenishing their body fat for the remainder of their long trip. Semipalmated Sandpipers migrate almost the entire length of the Americas, and they require that their migratory pit-stops provide ample food resources.

Although the Boston area does not host the abundance of Semis found along the windswept shores of Cape Cod and the southern islands, our wetlands and beaches are just as vital to the survival of smaller groups of these feathered delights. The shores of Nahant, Revere Beach and Winthrop Beach are good places to look for Semipalmated Sandpipers mixed among flocks of other shorebirds.

'Semipalmated' refers to the slight webbing between this bird's front toes. The scientific name *pusilla* is Latin for 'petty' or 'small.'

Similar Species: Western Sandpiper has a longer, slightly downcurved bill. Least Sandpiper (p. 61) has pale legs. Dunlin (p. 63) has a downcurved bill. White-rumped Sandpiper has an all-white rump and wings that extend beyond the tail.

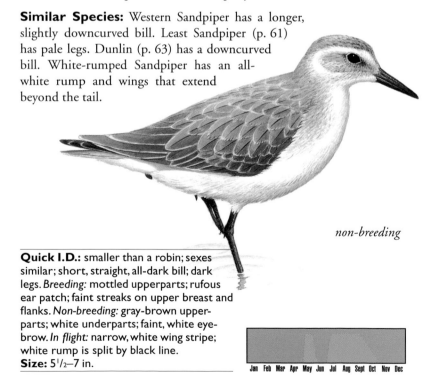

non-breeding

Quick I.D.: smaller than a robin; sexes similar; short, straight, all-dark bill; dark legs. *Breeding:* mottled upperparts; rufous ear patch; faint streaks on upper breast and flanks. *Non-breeding:* gray-brown upperparts; white underparts; faint, white eyebrow. *In flight:* narrow, white wing stripe; white rump is split by black line.
Size: 5¹/₂–7 in.

Jan Feb Mar Apr May Jun Jul Aug Sept Oct Nov Dec

Least Sandpiper
Calidris minutilla

The Least Sandpiper is the smallest of our shorebirds, but its size is not a deterrent to its migratory feats. Like most other 'peeps'—a term used to group the sometimes difficult to identify, small *Calidris* sandpipers—the Least Sandpipers passing through Boston migrate to the Arctic to breed.

Groups of these tiny birds can be seen on mudflats and beaches throughout our area. Their plumage matches perfectly with their preferred habitat, and it is usually their rapid movements that reveal these diminutive sprinters. Least Sandpipers tenaciously peck the moist substrate with their dexterous bills, eating mosquitoes, beach fleas, amphipods and other aquatic invertebrates.

Similar Species: Pectoral Sandpiper is larger and has a well-defined border on the breast. Other 'peeps' tend to have dark legs and are generally larger.

non-breeding

Jan Feb Mar Apr May Jun Jul Aug Sept Oct Nov Dec

Quick I.D.: sparrow-sized; sexes similar. *Adult:* black bill; yellow legs; dark, mottled back; buff-brown breast, head and nape; light breast streaking. *Immature:* like adult, but with faintly streaked breast.
Size: 5–6 in.

Purple Sandpiper

Calidris maritima

The rocky outcroppings and jetties of Winthrop Beach and Nahant provide excellent habitat for the daring Purple Sandpiper. Contrary to the implications of its 'sandpiper' name, this shorebird prefers to forage among the crashing waves on slippery rocks rather than on calm and sandy beaches. It is commonly seen in our area during the winter months, foraging along the intertidal zone for a delicious variety of mollusks, insects, crustaceans and aquatic plants. This bird is named for the subtle, usually unnoticeable purple tone on its back.

During the breeding season, this bird relies on the bounty of the brief arctic summer to raise its young among many dangers, including hunting Arctic Foxes, looting Long-tailed Jaegers and crushing Musk Oxen hooves. To avoid such dangers, sandpiper young have evolved with the ability to run and forage on their own immediately after birth.

Similar Species: Dunlin (p. 63) has dark legs and a longer, thicker bill; in breeding plumage it has a black belly and a reddish back; and in non-breeding plumage it has a grayish back.

non-breeding

Quick I.D.: smaller than a robin; sexes similar; long, drooping bill has orange-yellow base and black tip; orange-yellow legs; white wing stripe; dark central stripe on rump and tail; dull streaking on breast and flanks. *Breeding:* dark crown and back feathers are edged with tawny to rusty-brown highlights. *Non-breeding:* grayer plumage lacks rusty or tawny highlights.
Size: 9 in.

Jan Feb Mar Apr May Jun Jul Aug Sept Oct Nov Dec

Dunlin
Calidris alpina

non-breeding

Outside the breeding season, Dunlins are communal creatures that form swirling clouds of hundreds of individuals flying wing tip to wing tip, all changing course simultaneously, as if one entity. These hypnotic flights, which flash alternating shades of white and dark, are occasionally seen as Dunlins migrate along Boston's coastline. Watch for their peak migration in early May and throughout October.

The Dunlin, like many other shorebirds, nests on the arctic tundra and winters on the coasts of North America, Europe and Asia. Its tight flocks are generally more exclusive than many other shorebird troupes: few species mix with groups of Dunlins. This bird was originally called the 'Dunling' (meaning 'a small brown bird'), but for unknown reasons the 'g' was later dropped.

Similar Species: Least Sandpiper (p. 61) is smaller. Sanderling (p. 59) is paler and is usually seen running in the surf. Purple Sandpiper (p. 62) prefers rocky areas, and always has a pale belly, yellow legs and a yellow bill with a black tip.

Jan Feb Mar Apr May Jun Jul Aug Sept Oct Nov Dec

Quick I.D.: smaller than a robin; sexes similar; slightly downcurved bill; dark legs. *Breeding:* black belly; streaked underparts; rusty back. *Non-breeding:* pale gray underparts; grayish-brown upperparts.
Size: 8–9 in.

Short-billed Dowitcher
Limnodromus griseus

High tides force dowitchers and other wintering shorebirds to high, dry ground, often packing them together in large numbers. Dowitchers tend to be stockier than most shorebirds, and they avoid deeper water. The sewing machine–like rhythms that dowitchers perform while foraging deeply into the mudflats is helpful for field identification. Look for the Short-billed Dowitcher at Belle Isle and Point of Pines from the beginning of July to the end of August.

This bird can only be called 'short-billed' in comparison to its long-billed relative. Unfortunately, separating the two Boston-area dowitcher species is one of the most difficult tasks any birder can attempt, so most people are perfectly content to simply call them 'dowitchers.'

Similar Species: Long-billed Dowitcher has barring on its sides and an unmarked breast, its plumage is darker overall, and its bill is slightly longer. Common Snipe has longer legs, heavily barred upperparts and different foraging techniques.

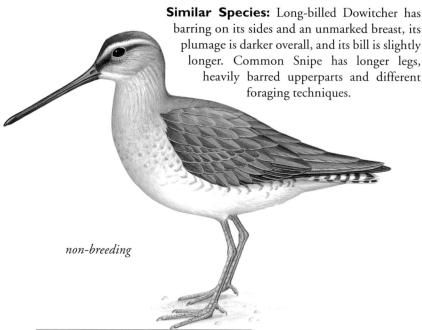

non-breeding

Quick I.D.: larger than a robin; sexes similar; very long, straight, dark bill; very stocky body; short neck. *Breeding:* reddish underparts; lightly barred flanks; dark, mottled upperparts; dark eye line; light eyebrow; dark yellow legs; white rump. *Non-breeding:* gray overall; white belly.
Size: 11–12¹/₂ in. (female larger).

Jan Feb Mar Apr May Jun Jul Aug Sept Oct Nov Dec

American Woodcock

Scolopax minor

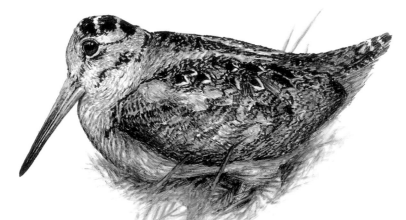

This well-camouflaged bird inhabits woods and thickets, such as at Maplecroft Farm in Ipswich and Daniel Webster Wildlife Sanctuary in Marshfield. For much of the year, the American Woodcock's behavior matches its cryptic and unassuming attire—its lifestyle does little to reveal itself to the outside world. For a short month each spring, however, male woodcocks explode into vanity.

The courtship performance begins when the male selects a clearing in the woods, where he gives a plaintive *bjeeent!* that inspires him into an Elvis-like boogie. Since the woodcock's legs are short, he usually selects a stage that is free of thick vegetation, which would block the females' views of his swinging strut. When he has sashayed sufficiently, he takes to the air. Spiraling upward into the evening sky, he twitters increasingly toward the sky-dance climax. Upon hitting the peak of his ascent, the male woodcock relaxes, and then he plummets, uncontrolled, to the ground. Just before impact, the woodcock pulls out of the crippled dive and alights on his dancing stage, where he resumes his breeding ballet. To attend this long-running musical, visit a moist woodland edge in April or May.

Similar Species: Common Snipe has a striped head and back and pointed wings.

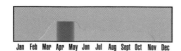

Jan Feb Mar Apr May Jun Jul Aug Sept Oct Nov Dec

Quick I.D.: jay-sized; sexes similar; chunky; very long bill; large eyes; rusty underparts. *In flight:* rounded wings.
Size: 10–12 in.

Laughing Gull

Larus atricilla

Imagine how fun it would be to fly over downtown Boston and watch the frantic urban antics of the people below. Maybe that is why the well-named Laughing Gull hurls its endless laugh across the city landscape. Of course, its raucous call might also be a triumphant expression of joy from overcoming hardship and near extermination. By the late 1800s, the high commercial demand for egg collections and feathers for women's hats nearly wiped out the breeding population of Laughing Gulls throughout New England. Fortunately, the efforts of a few dedicated people were enough to protect this bird in our area. More recently, however, Laughing Gull populations have been declining because of increased competition with the larger Herring Gulls and Great Black-backed Gulls.

Although Laughing Gulls do not breed in the Boston area—they nest primarily on Cape Cod—non-breeding birds and foraging adults are commonly seen in our area from April to October.

Similar Species: Bonaparte's Gull (p. 67) is smaller, has a black bill and orange feet and is more common in winter, when its head is mostly white with a black ear spot. Little Gull is smaller, and both it and the Black-headed Gull are seen in winter, when each has a white head with a black ear spot.

breeding

Quick I.D.: small gull; sexes similar; black head; red bill; black feet; incomplete, white eye ring; white neck and underparts; dark gray back; black-tipped wings.
Size: 16¹/₂ in.

Jan Feb Mar Apr May Jun Jul Aug Sept Oct Nov Dec

Bonaparte's Gull

Larus philadelphia

Their scratchy little calls accompany Bonaparte's Gulls as they forage along Boston's shorelines, commonly feeding on the water's surface and resting atop concrete platforms. The local Bonaparte's Gull population increases from April to early June as migrants pass through our area. Most are on their way to the northern boreal forest, where they nest, in most un-gull-like fashion, in spruce trees.

When Bonaparte's Gulls return to our area in late August, some remaining through December, they are more visible but far less striking in appearance. Most Bonaparte's Gulls lose their distinctive black hoods for winter, but they retain flashy white wing patches and a noticeable black spot behind the eye. Birders often search through flocks of Bonaparte's Gulls for their rarer cousins: Black-headed Gulls, Little Gulls or even Ross's Gulls.

This gull was not named after the famed French emperor, but after his nephew, Charles Lucien Bonaparte, who brought recognition to his family's name through the practice of ornithology.

Similar Species: Laughing Gull (p. 66) is larger and has black feet, black wing tips and a darker gray mantle, and adults have a red bill. Common Tern (p. 70) and Forster's Tern have forked tails and lack the white wing flash.

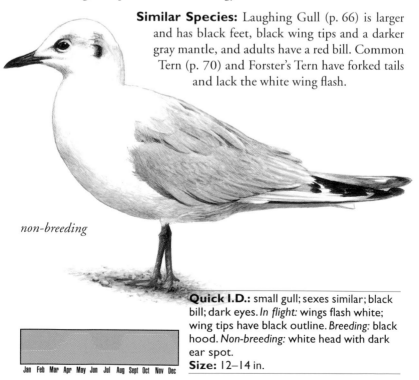

non-breeding

Quick I.D.: small gull; sexes similar; black bill; dark eyes. *In flight:* wings flash white; wing tips have black outline. *Breeding:* black hood. *Non-breeding:* white head with dark ear spot.

Size: 12–14 in.

Jan Feb Mar Apr May Jun Jul Aug Sept Oct Nov Dec

Herring Gull
Larus argentatus

Many gulls come and go in Boston, but the Herring Gull is a year-round resident, particularly along the coast. Although this familiar bird is commonly referred to as a 'seagull,' it does not rightfully deserve that moniker, as several other gulls are more closely tied to salt water. Large flocks of this gull can be found in bays, lakes, garbage dumps, shorelines, city parks and agricultural fields. Herring Gulls are so widely distributed that they are sure to be sighted on just about any birding trip taken around Boston Harbor, along the shores of the outer coast or through downtown Boston.

Like other large gulls, the Herring Gull takes four years to achieve adult plumage. It starts out dark brown, and each successive plumage more closely resembles that of the adult. Although it is often overlooked by even the most curious naturalist, the Herring Gull is an engineering marvel. Agile on land, an effortless flyer, wonderfully adaptive and with a stomach for anything digestible, the Herring Gull is an extraordinary bird that is worthy of our admiration.

Similar Species: Ring-billed Gull has yellow legs and a black band around the tip of the bill.

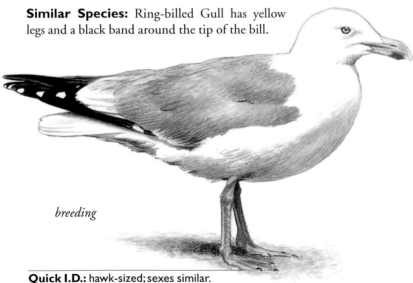

breeding

Quick I.D.: hawk-sized; sexes similar.
Adult: white head and body; gray back; pink legs; dark wing tips; yellow eyes; red spot on lower mandible (seen only at close range). *Immature:* variable; brown overall.
Size: 24–26 in.

Jan Feb Mar Apr May Jun Jul Aug Sept Oct Nov Dec

Great Black-backed Gull
Larus marinus

Surrounded by productive sources of fresh and salt water, and home to a few million food waste–generating humans, the Boston area is gull paradise. This is particularly true for North America's largest gull, the aggressive and dominating Great Black-backed Gull. A year-round resident, this bird is easily identified among other gulls of our city by its black mantle and commanding proportions.

This bird nests in large colonies each summer, usually near or among a nesting colony of Herring Gulls. Successful breeding colonies are usually situated on coastal islands or sea cliffs close to a reliable source of food and isolated from the threat of hungry mammals, such as skunks, weasels and foxes. Just as Great Black-backs avoid predatory mammals, many species of terns and other seabirds avoid the aggressive instinct of this formidable bird.

Similar Species: Herring Gull (p. 68) has light gray upperparts with black wing tips. Ring-billed Gull has yellow legs and a black band around the tip of the bill. Lesser Black-backed Gull has a dark gray back.

breeding

Quick I.D.: very large gull; sexes similar; white head, neck and underparts, except for gray underside of wings; black upper parts; pale pink legs; pale eyes; large yellow bill with red spot on lower mandible.
Size: 30 in.

Common Tern
Sterna hirundo

breeding

The Common Tern generally goes unnoticed until a splash draws attention to its headfirst dives into the water. Once it has firmly seized a small fish in its black-tipped bill, the tern bounces back into the air and continues its leisurely flight. Common Terns are easily observed in May as they work the shores of Squantum during migration. Although some terns remain to nest, many in three large colonies south of Boston, most choose to continue north for breeding opportunities.

Although terns and gulls share many of the same physical characteristics, there are features that clearly separate the two groups. Terns seldom rest on the water, and they rarely soar in flight, whereas gulls never plunge-dive into the water after fish. Also, terns have very short necks, pointed wings and long, forked tails, and they tend to look toward the ground during flight. Both gulls and terns tend to nest in similar regions, but this could be more convenient for the gulls, because they routinely prey on the smaller terns and their chicks.

Similar Species: Roseate Tern has red only at the base of the bill and has a much longer, forked tail. Caspian Tern has a large, red bill and is gull-sized. Forster's Tern has a grayer tail and frosted wing tips.

Quick I.D.: larger than a pigeon; sexes similar; black cap; orange or red bill tipped with black; gray back and wings; white throat and belly. *In flight:* pointed wings; forked tail; often hovers.
Size: 14–16 in.

Jan Feb Mar Apr May Jun Jul Aug Sept Oct Nov Dec

Least Tern
Sterna antillarum

On hot, sunny, summer weekends, one can appreciate the Least Tern's dilemma. Out-of-state tourists and Boston-area residents flock to crowded beaches, where finding a place to lay down your towel can be an exercise in futility. Although people visit Massachusetts's coastal beaches for pleasure, Least Terns are there out of necessity—they nest exclusively on open, sandy beaches. This tern's nest is a simple, hollow scrape in the sand. Provided that the nest is not raided by a predator or inadvertently destroyed by beach-goers, the one to three young will hatch in 20 to 25 days.

This threatened species is now restricted to breeding in a few scattered, protected areas, which are usually fenced off to protect them from humans. The courtship rituals of North America's smallest tern are quite elaborate, and they include pre-nuptial flights and feeding interactions. Terns are among the few animals (including humans) that present gifts to potential mates. With an increase in our awareness, it is possible that both humans and species like the Least Tern can share the rich asset of Massachusetts's beaches.

Similar Species: Forster's Tern, Caspian Tern and Common Tern (p. 70) are much larger, lack the white forehead and have red or orange bills.

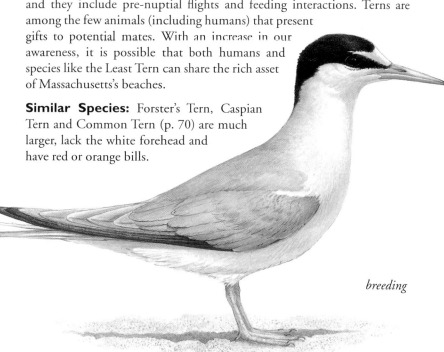

breeding

Jan Feb Mar Apr May Jun Jul Aug Sept Oct Nov Dec

Quick I.D.: robin-sized; sexes similar; black cap; white forehead; yellow bill with a black tip. *In flight:* long, tapered wings with black outer edges.
Size: 9–10 in.

Rock Dove
Columba livia

The ubiquitous urban Rock Dove, widely known as the 'Pigeon,' has taken advantage of humans for food and shelter. This Eurasian native lives in old buildings, on ledges and on bridges, and it feeds primarily on waste grain and human handouts. It was first brought to North America in 1606 as a food source, but it quickly became a popular pet. Rock Doves quickly dispersed from the East Coast to colonize the entire continent, with many birds returning to their ancestral habits of nesting on cliffs and surviving on wild seeds and berries.

Rock Doves might appear strained when they walk—their heads move back and forth with every step—but few birds are as agile in flight or as abundant in urban and industrial areas. Although no other bird varies as much in coloration, all Rock Doves, whether white, red, blue or mixed-pigment, will clap their wings above and below their bodies upon take-off.

Similar Species: Mourning Dove (p. 73) is the same length as the Rock Dove, but it is slender and has a long, tapering tail and olive-brown plumage.

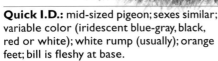

Quick I.D.: mid-sized pigeon; sexes similar; variable color (iridescent blue-gray, black, red or white); white rump (usually); orange feet; bill is fleshy at base.
Size: 13–14 in.

Jan Feb Mar Apr May Jun Jul Aug Sept Oct Nov Dec

Mourning Dove
Zenaida macroura

As a Mourning Dove bursts into flight, its wings 'clap' above and below its body for the first few wingbeats. The Mourning Dove is a swift, direct flier, and its wings can be heard whistling through the air. When it is not in flight, the Mourning Dove's peaceful *coooah-coooo-cooooo-coooo!* call can be heard filtering through open woodlands. These year-round residents roost inconspicuously in trees, but their soft cooing often betrays their presence.

The Mourning Dove feeds primarily on the ground in open areas, picking up seeds and the odd piece of grit to help grind down hard seed coatings. It builds a flat, loose stick nest that rests flimsily on branches and trunks. Mourning Doves are attentive parents, and, like other members of the pigeon family, they feed 'milk' to their young. It isn't true milk—birds don't have mammary glands—but a fluid produced by glands in the bird's crop. The chicks insert their bills down the adult's throat to drink the rich, thick liquid meal.

Similar Species: Rock Dove (p. 72) has a white rump, is stockier and has a shorter tail.

Quick I.D.: jay-sized; sexes similar; gray-brown plumage; long, white-trimmed, tapering tail; sleek body; dark, shiny patch below ear; orange feet; dark bill; buff-colored underparts.
Size: 11–13 in.

Jan Feb Mar Apr May Jun Jul Aug Sept Oct Nov Dec

Eastern Screech-Owl

Otus asio

Despite its small size, the Eastern Screech-Owl is a versatile hunter. It has a varied diet that ranges from insects, earthworms and fish to birds larger than itself. Silent and reclusive by day, screech-owls hunt at night. Strolling through the deciduous woodlands of Cherry Hill in Marshfield or the Glades in Cohasset during an early spring evening, a person with a keen ear will hear the distinctive, whistled, whinny voice of the Eastern Screech-Owl.

Most owls' senses are refined for darkness and their bodies for silence. Their large, forward-facing eyes have many times more light-gathering sensors than do ours, and the wings of nocturnal owls are edged with frayed feathers for silent flight. Their ears, which occupy a large part of the sides of their heads, are asymmetrical (one is higher than the other), which enables these birds to pinpoint sounds more easily. Given these adaptations, it is no surprise that owls have successfully invaded nearly all of the world's major ecosystems.

Similar Species: Northern Saw-whet Owl has a dark facial disc and no ear tufts.

gray phase

Quick I.D.: robin-sized; sexes similar; short, widely spaced ear tufts; heavy vertical streaking and bars on breast; yellow eyes; dark bill; two color phases (gray [more common] and red).
Size: 8–9 in. (female slightly larger).

Jan Feb Mar Apr May Jun Jul Aug Sept Oct Nov Dec

Great Horned Owl
Bubo virginianus

The Great Horned Owl is the most widely distributed owl in North America, and it is among the most formidable of predators. It uses specialized hearing, powerful talons and human-sized eyes during nocturnal hunts for mice, rabbits, birds, amphibians and occasionally fish. It has a poorly developed sense of smell, however, and it frequently preys on skunks—worn-out and discarded Great Horned Owl feathers are often identifiable by a simple sniff.

The deep, resonant hooting of the Great Horned Owl is easily imitated, often leading to interesting exchanges between bird and birder. The call's deep tone is not as distinctive as its pace, which closely follows the rhythm of *eat my food, I'll-eat yooou*. Like most owls, Great Horned Owls are quite capable of seeing and hunting during daylight hours, but they tend to hunt under lower light conditions when their prey seem to be more active and available to be snatched.

Similar Species: Eastern Screech-Owl (p. 74) is much smaller and has vertical breast streaking. Long-eared Owl has a slimmer body and vertical streaks on its breast, and its ear tufts are very close together.

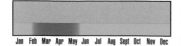

Jan Feb Mar Apr May Jun Jul Aug Sept Oct Nov Dec

Quick I.D.: hawk-sized; sexes similar; large, widely spaced ear tufts; fine, horizontal barring on breast; dark brown plumage; white throat.
Size: 18–25 in.

Common Nighthawk
Chordeiles minor

The Common Nighthawk has two distinct personalities: mild-mannered by day, it rests on the ground or on a horizontal tree branch, its color and shape blending perfectly into the texture of the bark; at dusk, it takes on a new form as a dazzling and erratic flyer, catching insects in flight. Accordingly, you are most likely to see this bird during its twilight hunting forays or its mid-August migration.

To many people, the sounds of nighthawks are the sounds of summer evenings, and the recent declines in their numbers have left many naturalists longing for their previously common calls. The fascinating courtship of Common Nighthawks occurs over forest openings, beaches and urban areas. The nighthawks repeatedly call out with a loud, nasal *peeent!* as they circle high overhead; then they dive suddenly toward the ground and create a hollow *vroom* by thrusting their wings forward at the last possible moment, pulling out of the dive.

Similar Species: Whip-poor-will (p. 77) has a rounded tail and wings.

♂

Quick I.D.: robin-sized; cryptic, light to dark brown plumage. *Male:* white throat. *Female:* buff throat. *In flight:* long, pointed wings; white wrist bands; shallowly forked tail; flight is erratic.
Size: 9–10 in.

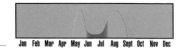

Jan Feb Mar Apr May Jun Jul Aug Sept Oct Nov Dec

Whip-poor-will

Caprimulgus vociferus

♂

The Whip-poor-will makes identification easy for novice birdwatchers because this nighttime hunter fills the evening with its own name. The distinctive *whip-poor-will* is chanted persistently, about once a second. A patient naturalist, John Burroughs, once counted 1088 consecutive calls from an individual, reinforcing this bird's apt scientific name, *vociferus* (a Latin word meaning 'voice-carrying').

The Whip-poor-will arrives in the Boston area by the end of May, quickly passing through our developed urban and suburban jungle to find an open woodland in which to nest. Although it is a difficult bird to meet during migration, the occasional bird makes an appearance at Mt. Auburn Cemetery in Cambridge or at Nahant Thicket. Once these birds arrive in suitable nesting territory, such as in Myles Standish State Forest, no nest is constructed; they simply lay their eggs on bare ground. These well-camouflaged birds also choose to roost on bare ground during the day, and at dusk they can occasionally be seen resting on or alongside roadsides.

Similar Species: Common Nighthawk (p. 76) has pointed wings, a notched tail and white wrist bands.

Quick I.D.: robin sized; gray-brown plumage; rounded wings and tail; black throat. *Male:* white 'necklace' and outer tail feathers. *Female:* buff 'necklace' and outer tail feathers.
Size: 9–10 in.

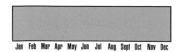

Jan Feb Mar Apr May Jun Jul Aug Sept Oct Nov Dec

Belted Kingfisher

Ceryle alcyon

The Belted Kingfisher is found near quiet waters, never far from shore. As the name suggests, kingfishers primarily prey on fish, which they catch with precise, headfirst dives. A dead branch extending over water will often serve as a perch from which they can survey the fish below.

The Belted Kingfisher builds its nest near the end of a long tunnel excavated a few feet into a sandy or dirt bank. A rattling call—similar to a teacup shaking on a saucer—blue-gray coloration and a large crest are the distinctive features of the Belted Kingfisher. In most birds the males are more colorful, but female kingfishers are distinguished from males by the presence of a second, rust-colored band across the belly.

Although there are many species of kingfishers in the world, the Belted Kingfisher is the only member of its family across most of the United States. Where open water is found in the Boston area, Belted Kingfishers can often be encountered crashing into calm waters in search of fish.

Similar Species: Blue Jay (p. 90) is superficially similar.

Quick I.D.: pigeon-sized; blue-gray back, wings and head; shaggy crest; heavy bill. *Male:* single, blue breast band. *Female:* blue breast band and rust-colored 'belt.'
Size: 12–14 in.

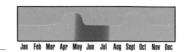

Jan Feb Mar Apr May Jun Jul Aug Sept Oct Nov Dec

Downy Woodpecker
Picoides pubescens

Soft taps carry through a quiet forest, sounding out the activities of a Downy Woodpecker. It methodically searches for hidden invertebrates by chipping off dead bark and probing into crevices. This woodpecker's small bill is amazingly effective at removing tiny slabs of bark, which rain down to the forest floor. The Downy Woodpecker is a systematic forager, and because of its small bill, it can find food where larger-billed woodpeckers cannot reach. Often, it is only when all the nooks of a tree have been probed that the Downy will look about and give a chipper note before moving on to explore neighboring trees.

This black-and-white bird is the smallest North American woodpecker, and it is common in most woodlots, city parks and neighborhoods with a good population of trees. Backyard feeders filled with suet are especially attractive to this friendly and trusting delight. The male is readily distinguished from the female by a small patch of red feathers on the back of his head.

Similar Species: Hairy Woodpecker is larger and has a longer bill and clean white outer tail feathers.

Jan Feb Mar Apr May Jun Jul Aug Sept Oct Nov Dec

Quick I.D.: large sparrow–sized; black-and-white wings and back; unmarked, white underparts; short, stubby bill; white outer tail feathers are spotted black. *Male:* red patch on back of head. *Female:* no red patch.
Size: 6–7 in.

Northern Flicker
Colaptes auratus

Walkers strolling through any of our larger parks might be surprised by a woodpecker flushing from the ground before them. As the Northern Flicker beats a hasty retreat, it reveals an unmistakable white rump and yellow wing linings. It is the least arboreal of our woodpeckers, and it spends much of its time feeding on the ground. Often, it is only when the Northern Flicker is around its nest cavity in a tree that it truly behaves like other woodpeckers: clinging, rattling and drumming.

The Northern Flicker can be seen year-round in the wilder parts of the city. It occasionally visits backyard feeders, and is less abundant through our winters. The Northern Flicker, like some other birds, has the peculiar, but ingenious, habit of squashing ants and then preening itself with the remains. Ants contain concentrations of formic acid, which is believed to kill small parasites living on the flicker's skin and in its feathers.

Similar Species: Red-bellied Woodpecker has a red crown and black and white bars on its back.

Quick I.D.: jay-sized; brown-barred back; spotted underparts; black bib; white rump; long bill; yellow wing and tail linings; gray crown; red nape. *Male:* black mustache. *Female:* no mustache.
Size: 11–14 in.

Ruby-throated Hummingbird
Archilochus colubris

You are fortunate if you manage to get a prolonged look at a Ruby-throated Hummingbird, the only eastern hummingbird. Most meetings are over before they begin—a loud hum draws your attention to a small object zinging about, but it quickly disappears through the trees. It's often only after the bird has disappeared that its identity is realized.

Fortunately, Ruby-throated Hummingbirds are easily attracted to feeders of sweetened water (one part white sugar to four parts water). The male's iridescent ruby throat and emerald back play with the sunlight in ever-switching colors. The Ruby-throated Hummingbird's gentle appearance is misleading, however, and these fiercely aggressive birds will chase intruders away in spirited defense of a food source or prospective mates.

Hummingbirds are among the few birds able to fly vertically and in reverse. They can even flip backward and briefly fly upside-down to escape approaching danger. Amazingly, the wings of a hummingbird beat up to 80 times a second, and its heart can beat up to 1200 times a minute—compare that to our feeble 60- to 120-beat-per-minute hearts!

Similar Species: No birds, but possibly a hawkmoth.

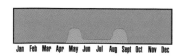

Jan Feb Mar Apr May Jun Jul Aug Sept Oct Nov Dec

Quick I.D.: our smallest bird; iridescent green back; long, thin, dark bill.
Male: iridescent ruby throat.
Size: 4 in.

Willow Flycatcher

Empidonax traillii

From its swaying willow perch, the Willow Flycatcher sings its chipper *fitz-bew* while surveying its chosen territory. Look for it in brushy and marshy lowland areas in and around Boston. Nahant Thicket, Sudbury River Valley and Lynnfield Marsh are all good places to observe this feisty sprite.

Boston is an exceptionally rich area for flycatchers; the Willow, Least, Alder, Acadian and Yellow-bellied flycatchers can all be seen here. Empidonax flycatchers (named after their genus) occur throughout North America, and they are famous in birdwatching circles for being hard to identify. Their plumages have slight variations that are obvious only under ideal conditions, but they can best be distinguished from each other by voice and habitat.

Similar Species: Least, Alder, Acadian and Yellow-bellied flycatchers all have distinctive, simple calls: Least sings *che-bek, che-bek, che-bek*; Alder sings a spunky *free-beer*; Acadian gives a forceful *peet-sah*; Yellow-bellied offers an even *che-bunk*.

Quick I.D.: sparrow-sized; sexes similar; olive-green overall; faint white eye ring; two wing bars; dark bill; yellow wash on belly; dark wings and tail.
Size: 5–6 in.

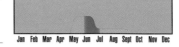

Jan Feb Mar Apr May Jun Jul Aug Sept Oct Nov Dec

Eastern Phoebe

Sayornis phoebe

breeding

Although many birds pump their tails while they are perched, no bird can match the zest and frequency of the Eastern Phoebe's tail wag. This early spring migrant might lack a distinctive plumage, but its identity is never questioned when the quick and jerky tail rises and falls. Keeping in perfect synchrony with its rhythmic rump, the Eastern Phoebe's voice joins in accompaniment—as its name suggests, this small flycatcher bolts out a cheery *fee-bee* from an exposed spring perch.

The Eastern Phoebe is one of the first songbirds to return to Boston in spring, and it frequently builds its nest on buildings. Phoebes might re-use the same nest site for several years, or they might choose a new site annually. Whatever the case, the Eastern Phoebe's nest is always protected from the rain by a roof—often a bridge, since it likes to nest near streams. If you're lucky, you could even find a phoebe nesting out by your backyard shed!

Similar Species: Willow Flycatcher (p. 82) and other empidonax flycatchers are smaller and have wing bars. Eastern Wood-Pewee has wing bars and a different voice, and it doesn't wag its tail.

Jan Feb Mar Apr May Jun Jul Aug Sept Oct Nov Dec

Quick I.D.: larger than a sparrow; sexes similar; brownish-gray back; no wing bars or eye ring; dark tail, wings and head. *Breeding:* white belly. *Non-breeding:* yellowish belly.
Size: 6¹/₂–7 in.

Great Crested Flycatcher
Myiarchus crinitus

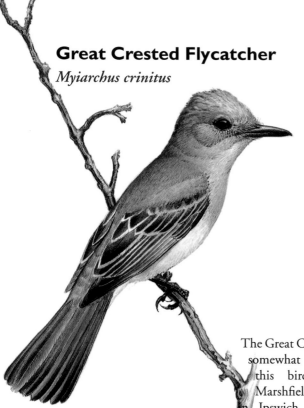

The Great Crested Flycatcher's name is somewhat misleading. A glimpse of this bird at Cherry Hill in Marshfield, Willowdale State Forest in Ipswich or in any Boston-area woodland will leave the observer with the impression that it is a 'Great Flycatcher.' Closer inspection of the bird might reveal a small crest, but certainly nothing to rival a Blue Jay or Northern Cardinal.

The Great Crested Flycatcher has an unusual taste in decor for its nest cavity—it occasionally lays a shed snakeskin as a doormat. This uncommon, but noteworthy, practice can identify the nest of this flycatcher, the only member of its family in our area to nest in a cavity. The purpose of the snakeskin is not known, but it seems to be important enough that more versatile Great Crested Flycatchers have occasionally substituted plastic wrap for reptilian skin.

Similar Species: Eastern Wood-Pewee, Eastern Phoebe (p. 83) and other flycatchers are smaller and lack the lemon yellow belly and the chestnut tail lining.

Quick I.D.: smaller than a robin; sexes similar; yellow belly; gray throat and head; dark back and wings; chestnut tail lining; rufous wing linings; erect crest.
Size: 7–8 in.

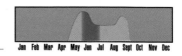

Jan Feb Mar Apr May Jun Jul Aug Sept Oct Nov Dec

Eastern Kingbird

Tyrannus tyrannus

When one thinks of a tyrant, the image of a menacing ruler or a large carnivorous dinosaur are much more likely to come to mind than that of a little bird. Initially, the Eastern Kingbird might not seem as imposing as other known tyrants, but this flycatcher certainly lives up to its scientific name, *Tyrannus tyrannus*. The Eastern Kingbird is pugnacious—it will fearlessly attack crows, hawks, other large birds and even people that pass through its territory. The intruders are often vigorously pursued, pecked and plucked for some distance until the kingbird is satisfied that there is no further threat.

The courtship flight of the Eastern Kingbird, which can easily be seen in local fields and shrubby areas, is characterized by short, quivering wingbeats. It is a touching display, even for this flattering little tyrant.

Similar Species: Tree Swallow (p. 88) and all other flycatchers lack the white, terminal tail band and are not black and white.

Jan Feb Mar Apr May Jun Jul Aug Sept Oct Nov Dec

Quick I.D.: smaller than a robin; sexes similar; black head, back, wings and tail; white underparts; white, terminal tail band; orange-red crown (rarely seen).
Size: 9 in.

Chimney Swift
Chaetura pelagica

The Chimney Swift is one of the frequent fliers of the bird world—only raising a family keeps this bird off its wings—and it feeds, drinks, bathes and even mates in flight. During its four- to five-year average life span, this aeronaut can travel more than one million miles. Swifts often forage for flying insects at great heights, and during the height of the day they are often visible only as specks in the sky. As the sun sinks to the horizon, however, flocks of Chimney Swifts can be seen spiraling to their evening roosts, casting a distinct boomerang silhouette as they glide.

When they are not in flight, swifts use their small but strong claws to cling precariously to vertical surfaces. Chimney Swifts nest in cavities, and because many old, hollow hardwood trees have been removed in the past few centuries, Chimney Swifts have adopted human structures, such as chimneys, as common nesting sites. Recently, Chimney Swift populations have been declining, and it isn't clear whether the problems are on their breeding or wintering grounds.

Similar Species: All swallows have smooth, direct flight and broader wings.

Quick I.D.: smaller than a sparrow; sexes similar; brown overall; slim. *In flight:* rapid wingbeats; erratic flight; boomerang-shaped profile.
Size: 5¹/₂ in.

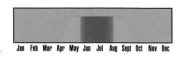

Jan Feb Mar Apr May Jun Jul Aug Sept Oct Nov Dec

Purple Martin

Progne subis

Late summer is a very busy time around a Purple Martin complex. Adults spiral around the large, communal nest box, coming and going in foraging forays. The year's young perch at the openings, impatiently waiting for their parents to return with mouthfuls of flying insects. A patient observer will notice how orderly the apparent confusion is to the martin, and how efficiently the crowded complex is negotiated.

A Purple Martin complex should be placed high on a pole in the middle of a large, open area. The complex should be cleaned and plugged up after the martins have left, until they return in spring. If you fail to perform these annual procedures, House Sparrows and European Starlings will gladly and ruthlessly take over the complex before the preferred tenants return in spring.

Contrary to some advertising claims that martins will eat millions of mosquitoes, a martin colony can actually have the opposite effect. Martins eat dragonflies and damselflies, which are the true mosquito-eaters.

Similar Species: Barn Swallow (p. 89) has a deeply forked tail. Tree Swallow (p. 88) has a white belly. European Starling (p. 117) has a long bill and a short tail.

Jan Feb Mar Apr May Jun Jul Aug Sept Oct Nov Dec

Quick I.D.: smaller than a robin; pointed wings; forked tail; small bill. *Male:* deep, glossy blue plumage. *Female* and *Immature:* gray underparts; dull blue back.
Size: 7–8 in.

Tree Swallow

Tachycineta bicolor

Depending on food availability, Tree Swallows might forage for great distances, darting above open fields and wetlands as they catch flying insects in their bills. These bicolored birds occasionally swoop down to the water's surface for a quick mid-flight drink and bath. In bad weather, Tree Swallows might fly up to five miles to distant marshes or lakes to find flying insects in more suitable weather.

The Tree Swallow is among the first migrants to arrive in the Boston area, often beating the onset of warm spring weather. It returns to freshwater marshes by late March to begin its reproductive cycle in late April. It nests in abandoned woodpecker cavities as well as in nest boxes. When the parents leave their eggs for long periods of time, they cover them with feathers to keep them warm. By tossing feathers into the wind near nest-building birds, naturalists can enjoy close-up views of these birds as they swoop down.

Similar Species: Chimney Swift (p. 86) has slimmer wings and a darker belly. Northern Rough-winged Swallow has brown upperparts and a brown wash on the throat. Bank Swallow has brown upperparts and a brown breast band.

Quick I.D.: sparrow-sized; sexes similar; white underparts; small bill; small feet. *Adult:* iridescent blue-green upperparts; dark rump. *Immature:* brown upperparts. *In flight:* long, pointed wings; shallowly forked tail.
Size: 5–6 in.

Jan Feb Mar Apr May Jun Jul Aug Sept Oct Nov Dec

Barn Swallow

Hirundo rustica

The Barn Swallow has one of the longest migration routes of any North American land bird—many Barn Swallows winter in Argentina—but you cannot imagine a bird better adapted to the challenge. Barn Swallows fly effortlessly, expressing their aerial dominion with each stroke of their wings.

The Barn Swallow builds its cup-shaped mud nest in the eaves of barns, picnic shelters or any other structure that provides protection from the rain. It is not uncommon for a nervous parent bird to dive repeatedly at human 'intruders,' encouraging them to retreat. Occasionally, a nesting pair of birds can learn to trust their human neighbors, tolerating close, non-threatening visits.

The Barn Swallow is the only swallow in Boston to have a 'swallow tail,' and because it often forages at low altitudes, its deeply forked tail is easily observed.

Similar Species: Purple Martin (p. 87) has a shorter tail and lacks the russet throat and forehead. Cliff Swallow has the same colors overall, but it has a russet rump and a squared-off tail.

Quick I.D.: larger than a sparrow; sexes similar, but female is a bit duller; deeply forked tail; glossy blue back, wings and tail; buffy underparts; russet throat and forehead.
Size: 6–8 in.

Jan Feb Mar Apr May Jun Jul Aug Sept Oct Nov Dec

Blue Jay

Cyanocitta cristata

The wooded suburbs of Boston, with their broken forests and plentiful birdfeeders, must look a lot like Blue Jay heaven. One of our region's most identifiable birds—with its loud *jay-jay-jay* call, its blue, black and white plumage and its large crest—the Blue Jay is familiar to anyone with a generous supply of sunflower seeds or peanuts at their birdfeeder. Blue Jays are intelligent, aggressive and adaptable birds that don't hesitate to drive smaller birds, squirrels or even cats away when they feel threatened.

The Blue Jay represents all the admirable virtues and aggressive qualities of the corvid family, which includes crows and ravens. Beautiful, resourceful and vocally diverse, the Blue Jay can also be one of the most annoying and mischievous birds, and no predator is too formidable for this bird to harass. With their noisy calls, Blue Jays wake up neighborhoods and forests where they are the self-appointed guardians. Fortunately, this colorful bird's extroverted character and boldness outweigh its occasional, briefly annoying behavior.

Similar Species: Eastern Bluebird (p. 99) is smaller, lacks a crest and has a reddish belly.

Quick I.D.: larger than a robin; sexes similar; blue crest, back, wings and tail; black 'necklace' and lore; white wing bars; light belly.
Size: 11–12 in.

Jan Feb Mar Apr May Jun Jul Aug Sept Oct Nov Dec

American Crow
Corvus brachyrhynchos

It has been suggested that if humans were given feathers and flight, few would be as intelligent as crows. Scientific studies have shown that crows are capable of solving simple problems, which comes as no surprise to anyone who has watched a crow snip open garbage bags with scissors-like precision.

The American Crow calls with the classic, long, descending *caaaw*, either singly or in a series. Throughout the year, this common bird announces the start of the day to Boston-area residents. In late summer and fall, when their reproductive duties are completed, crows group together to roost in flocks, known as 'murders.' The crow population seems to have increased in our area, particularly during recent winters, and large flocks can be seen almost anywhere throughout Greater Boston.

The Boston area is also home to the virtually identical Fish Crow—a slightly smaller and more coastal-dwelling relative. The Fish Crow is most likely to be seen along the ocean coast scavenging for crustaceans, fish, food-waste or the eggs of gulls, terns and herons.

Similar Species: Fish Crow is best distinguished by its more nasal, double-noted *eh-eh* call.

Jan Feb Mar Apr May Jun Jul Aug Sept Oct Nov Dec

Quick I.D.: small gull–sized; sexes similar; all black; fan-shaped tail; slim overall.
Size: 18–20 in.

Black-capped Chickadee
Poecile atricapillus

Our state bird, the Black-capped Chickadee is one of the most common and endearing birds of Boston's urban and forested areas. Small, wandering flocks of chickadees seem to go out of their way to greet people strolling through city parks or relaxing in wooded backyards. Brave and adaptable year-round residents, chickadees spend much of the year moving about in loose groups, investigating nooks and crannies for food and uttering their delicate, cheery *chick-a-dee-dee-dee* calls. The chickadees are often joined by other birds, such as nuthatches, kinglets, creepers, Downy Woodpeckers and migrating warblers.

In spring and summer, Black-capped Chickadees seem strangely absent from our city parks and wooded ravines. They tend to remain inconspicuous while they are busily tending to their reproductive duties. Once the first fall chill arrives, however, the woods are once again vibrant with their busy activities and friendly antics.

Similar Species: Tufted Titmouse (p. 93) has a gray crest and lacks the black cap and bib. White-breasted Nuthatch (p. 94) lacks the black chin and has a short tail and a long bill. Blackpoll Warbler (p. 112) is a migrant with orange legs and streaked underparts.

Quick I.D.: smaller than a sparrow; sexes similar; black cap and bib; white cheeks; grayish back, wings and tail; light underparts.
Size: 5–6 in.

Jan Feb Mar Apr May Jun Jul Aug Sept Oct Nov Dec

Tufted Titmouse
Baeolophus bicolor

On a breaking spring day, an inquisitive Tufted Titmouse whistles *peter peter peter* from its perch, a short flight away from a well-stocked backyard feeder. For much of the year, the Tufted Titmouse is a familiar neighbor in many Boston-area communities—gracing backyards with its trusting inquisitions—although it is a relatively recent arrival in our area. The cause of the titmouse's expansion northward isn't known—it could be global warming or the spread of backyard birdfeeders, or perhaps a bit of both.

Tufted Titmice can be found nesting in most woodlands. They choose abandoned cavities, previously occupied and excavated by small woodpeckers, in which to build their nests. To make their borrowed homes cozy, titmice line their nests with hair boldly plucked from dogs, wild animals or even humans. If you take the hair accumulated in your hairbrush and set it out in your yard, it might attract a few of these curious birds, who will gladly incorporate a small part of you into the wildness of your neighborhood.

Similar Species: Cedar Waxwing (p. 120) also has a crest, but it is more brown than gray and has a black face mask and a yellow tail tip.

Quick I.D.: sparrow-sized; sexes similar; small crest; dark gray upperparts; light gray underparts; reddish flanks; small black spot on forehead.

Size: 5–6 in.

Jan Feb Mar Apr May Jun Jul Aug Sept Oct Nov Dec

White-breasted Nuthatch

Sitta carolinensis

The White-breasted Nuthatch is a curious bird. To the novice birdwatcher, the sight of a nuthatch calling repeatedly while it clings to the underside of a branch might seem odd. To a nuthatch, however, this gravity-defying act is as natural as flight. These tree-trunk acrobats make their seemingly dangerous headfirst hops look easy and routine. A nuthatch will frequently pause in mid-descent, arching its head out at right angles to the trunk and giving its distinctive and often repeated nasal call: *anh-anh-anh-anh.*

White-breasted Nuthatches frequently visit backyard feeders during invasions of Black-capped Chickadees, Tufted Titmice, House Sparrows and Blue Jays. At these busy times, you will notice their brilliant strategy of avoiding conflict: nuthatches fly in to the feeder, quickly pick out a sunflower seed and then disappear into the surrounding trees. There they scale the bark until they find a crevice in which to store their meal for later consumption. You can also attract nuthatches by hanging a suet feeder from one of your backyard trees during winter.

Similar Species: Red-breasted Nuthatch has a red breast and a black eye line. Black-capped Chickadee (p. 92) has a black bib and a longer tail.

♂

Quick I.D.: sparrow-sized; white cheeks and breast; steel blue back, wings and tail; straight bill; short tail; russet undertail coverts. *Male:* black cap. *Female:* grayish cap.
Size: 6 in.

Jan Feb Mar Apr May Jun Jul Aug Sept Oct Nov Dec

Carolina Wren

Thryothorus ludovicianus

Strong through the southern states, these persistent birds continue to push the limits of their range northward into Massachusetts, blessing Bostonians with their lively songs and chatter. Carolina Wrens can mate for life, and a pair will sing their unique 'duet' year-round as they forage for food and protect their valuable nesting territory.

Boston is currently recognized as the extreme northern limit of this bird's range, and even in years of mild winter weather, Carolina Wrens are yet to be met with regularity. A single cold winter of freezing temperatures and ice-rain can decimate the entire population of Carolina Wrens in Massachusetts, forcing them to attempt re-colonization under warmer circumstances. Boston-area residents can help this feathered delight hold its place in our area by maintaining birdfeeders tailored to the tastes of this charming bird—Carolina Wrens are particularly fond of suet and sunflower seeds.

Similar Species: House Wren (p. 96) and Winter Wren lack the prominent white eyebrow. Marsh Wren (p. 97) has a white-streaked, black triangular patch on its back.

Jan Feb Mar Apr May Jun Jul Aug Sept Oct Nov Dec

Quick I.D.: sparrow-sized; sexes similar; rusty brown upperparts; deep buff–colored underparts; white throat; long, prominent, white eyebrow.

Size: 5 1/2 in.

House Wren
Troglodytes aedon

This common bird of suburbs, city parks and woodlands sings as though its lungs were bottomless. The sweet, warbling song of the House Wren is distinguished by its melodious tone and its uninterrupted endurance. Although the House Wren is far smaller than a sparrow, it offers an unending song in one breath.

The House Wren is often seen from May to October in woodlands, city parks and backyards, skulking beneath the dense understory. Like all wrens, it frequently carries its short tail cocked straight up. The House Wren treats Boston-area neighborhoods to a few weeks of wonderful warbles in spring before it channels its energy to the task of reproduction. A male House Wren will fill up to a dozen nestboxes or other cavities with twigs for his mate, who will then line one of those nests with grass before laying her eggs.

Similar Species: Winter Wren's tail is shorter than its legs. Carolina Wren (p. 95) is larger and has a white eyebrow. Marsh Wren (p. 97) has white streaking on its back.

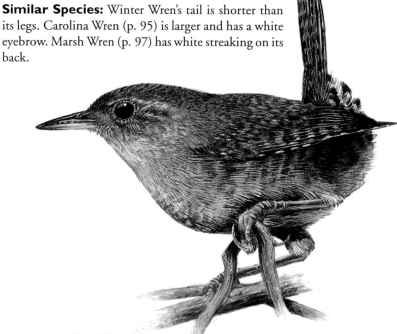

Quick I.D.: smaller than a sparrow; sexes similar; brown; tail is often cocked up; slightly downcurved bill; tail is as long as legs.
Size: 5 in.

Jan Feb Mar Apr May Jun Jul Aug Sept Oct Nov Dec

Marsh Wren
Cistothorus palustris

This energetic little bird usually lives in cattail marshes and dense, wet meadows bordered by willows. Although it usually sings from the deep vegetation, its distinctive voice is one of the characteristic sounds of our freshwater wetlands and saltwater marshes. In early spring, Great Meadows National Wildlife Refuge and the shores of the North River in Marshfield ring with the dynamic call of this reclusive bird. Its boisterous song has the repetitive, unnatural quality of an old sewing machine. Once you learn the rhythm, you will hear it whenever you visit many of our local wetlands.

A typical sighting of a Marsh Wren is to spot a brown blur moving noisily about within the shoreline tangles. Although this wren could be less than three yards from the observer, its cryptic habits and appearance are effective camouflage. Patient observers might be rewarded with a brief glimpse of a Marsh Wren perching high atop a cattail reed as it quickly evaluates its territory.

Similar Species: Winter, Carolina (p. 95) and House (p. 96) wrens all have unstreaked backs and generally avoid wetlands.

Jan Feb Mar Apr May Jun Jul Aug Sept Oct Nov Dec

Quick I.D.: smaller than a sparrow; sexes similar; brown overall; white streaking on back; white eye line; light throat and breast; cocked-up tail.
Size: 4–5 1/2 in.

Golden-crowned Kinglet

Regulus satrapa

The high-pitched, tinkling voice of a Golden-crowned Kinglet is as familiar as the sweet smell of coniferous forests. During late March and early April and then again in late September and early October, Boston's parks and older communities come alive with the Golden-crowned Kinglet's faint, high-pitched *tsee-tsee-tsee-tsee*. Kinglets are widespread, but not as common, in Boston through winter.

Although this bird is not immediately obvious to the uninformed passerby, a birdwatcher with a keen ear, patience and the willingness to draw down this smallest of North American songbirds with squeaks and pishes will encounter kinglets on many outdoor trips. As these tiny birds descend in loose flocks around a curious onlooker, their indistinct plumage and voice offer little excitement. When the flock circles nearby, however, flashing their regal crowns as they use the branches as swings and trapezes, the magic of these kinglets will emerge.

Similar Species: Ruby-crowned Kinglet has a reddish crown without a black outline and without the white eyebrow.

Quick I.D.: smaller than a sparrow; plump; dark olive back; white wing bars; dark tail and wings; white eyebrow. *Male:* fiery orange crown bordered by black. *Female:* lemon yellow crown bordered by black. **Size:** 4 in.

Jan Feb Mar Apr May Jun Jul Aug Sept Oct Nov Dec

Eastern Bluebird

Sialia sialis

Dressed with the colors of the cool sky on his back and the warm setting sun on his breast, the male Eastern Bluebird looks like a piece of pure sky come to life. To fully appreciate this lovely bird, try to spot a male as he sets up his territory on a crisp, early spring morning. Look for him in open country in Daniel Webster Wildlife Sanctuary in Marshfield, Broadmoor Wildlife Sanctuary in Natick and many other rural settings in the Boston area.

The Eastern Bluebird lost many of its natural nesting sites to House Sparrows and European Starlings and to the removal of dead trees from eastern Massachusetts. Concerned residents rallied for this bird, however, and they put up thousands of nest boxes to compensate for the losses. The Eastern Bluebird population has slowly increased as a result, and the vigilant residents have been rewarded with the regular sight of this bird's beautiful plumage against the local landscape.

Similar Species: Male Indigo Bunting (p. 141) lacks the red breast and has a conical bill. Blue Jay (p. 90) has a crest and is blue, black and white. Tree Swallow (p. 88), which often nests in bluebird boxes, has an iridescent blue-green back and white underparts.

Quick I.D.: smaller than a robin; thin bill; white undertail coverts. *Male:* blue back; red throat and breast. *Female:* less intense colors.

Size: 6–7 in.

Jan Feb Mar Apr May Jun Jul Aug Sept Oct Nov Dec

Veery

Catharus fuscescens

Like a tumbling waterfall, the Veery's voice descends with a liquid ripple. Like all other thrushes, it is a master of melodies, and it offers its unequaled songs to forests darkened by the setting sun. Listen for its aural treat during the last weeks of May in Willowdale State Forest in Ipswich or the cedar swamp remnants along Cedar Street in Bridgewater.

The Veery is perhaps the most terrestrial of Boston's thrushes, and it frequently nests on the ground. In characteristic thrush style, it searches for grubs and caterpillars by shuffling through loose leaf litter. When it finds an invertebrate delicacy, the Veery swallows it quickly and, ever-vigilant, cautiously looks about before renewing the hunt.

Similar Species: Wood (p. 101), Hermit and Swainson's thrushes and Ovenbird (p. 114) are more boldly patterned on the breast, each has a characteristic song, and none has the uniformly rufous upperparts from the head through the tail.

Quick I.D.: smaller than a robin; sexes similar; reddish-brown head, back, rump and tail; faint spotting on throat; inconspicuous eye ring.
Size: 7–8 in.

Jan Feb Mar Apr May Jun Jul Aug Sept Oct Nov Dec

Wood Thrush
Hylocichla mustelina

The Wood Thrush's musical warble—*Will you live with me? Way up high in a tree, I'll come right down and...seeee!*—has sadly faded from many areas of eastern Massachusetts. The Wood Thrush was once the voice of our area's hardwood forests, but it has declined because of forest fragmentation. Broken forests invite common open-area predators and parasites, such as skunks, foxes, crows, jays and cowbirds, which traditionally had little access to Wood Thrush nests insulated deep within the protected confines of vast hardwoods.

Like the hope and faith that seem to flow with the Wood Thrush's melody, the future might still hold promise for this often-glorified songbird. As the pioneer farms are slowly abandoned and society learns to value the sanctity of a bird song, the wild spirit of the Wood Thrush offers up an optimistic note.

Similar Species: Hermit Thrush lacks the black spots on the breast and has a reddish rump and tail. Veery (p. 100) and Swainson's Thrush lack the bold, black breast spots and the reddish head. Ovenbird (p. 114) has brown upperparts and a russet crown bordered by black.

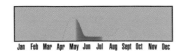

Jan Feb Mar Apr May Jun Jul Aug Sept Oct Nov Dec

Quick I.D.: smaller than a robin; sexes similar; large black spots on white breast; reddish-brown head, brown rump and tail; white eye ring; plump.
Size: 7¹/₂–8¹/₂ in.

American Robin

Turdus migratorius

If not for its abundance, the American Robin's voice and plumage would inspire pause and praise from casual onlookers. Acclimatization has dealt the robin an unfair hand, however, and this bird is under-appreciated for the pleasures it offers the eyes and ears of Boston-area residents. A robin dashing around a yard in search of worms or ripe berries is as familiar to many people as its three-part *cheerily-cheery up-cheerio* song. The American Robin's close relationship with urban areas has allowed many residents an insight into a bird's life. Their lively songs, their spotted young and occasionally even their deaths are experiences shared by their human neighbors.

American Robins appear to be year-round residents in Boston, but the bird dashing on your lawn in June might not be the same bird that shivers in February along the Charles River. Unnoticed by most Bostonians, the neighborhood robins take seasonal shifts: a few new birds arrive from the north just as most of the summer residents depart for southern climes in fall.

Similar Species: Other thrushes can resemble an immature robin, but robins always have at least a hint of red in the breast.

Quick I.D.: smaller than a jay; dark head, back and tail; yellow bill; striped throat; white undertail coverts. *Male:* brick red breast; darker hood. *Female:* slightly more orange breast; lighter hood.
Size: 9–11 in.

Jan Feb Mar Apr May Jun Jul Aug Sept Oct Nov Dec

Blue-headed Vireo

Vireo solitarius

The distinctive 'spectacles' of the Blue-headed Vireo identify this songbird as it forages purposefully along branches for insects. The white 'frames' are among the boldest of eye rings belonging to songbirds. During courtship, male Blue-headed Vireos fluff out their yellow flanks and bob ceremoniously to their prospective mates. The slow, high-pitched *look up … see me … here I am* song is rich in quality, and it is commonly heard in our area.

When it comes to building a nest, all vireos tend to share the same floorplan. They choose a horizontal fork in a tree and build a hanging, basket-like cup nest with grass, roots and spider silk. These characteristic nests are usually quite easy to spot once the leaves have fallen from the trees and the birds have departed to the south.

This lively bird was previously known as the Solitary Vireo, until scientists discovered that the eastern, Blue-headed form was genetically distinct from the western Cassin's form and the Plumbeous form of the Rocky Mountains.

Similar Species: Warbling Vireo and Red-eyed Vireo (p. 104) both lack the white 'spectacles.' White-eyed Vireo and Yellow-throated Vireo have yellow 'spectacles.'

Quick I.D.: sparrow-sized; sexes similar; white 'spectacles'; two whitish-yellow wing bars; gray head; green back; white underparts; yellow flanks; dark tail; stout bill; dark legs.
Size: 5–6 in.

Jan Feb Mar Apr May Jun Jul Aug Sept Oct Nov Dec

Red-eyed Vireo
Vireo olivaceus

breeding

The Red-eyed Vireo is the undisputed champion of singing endurance. During the breeding season, males sing from tall deciduous trees throughout the day. While most songbirds stop their courting melodies five or six hours after sunrise, the Red-eyed Vireo seems to gain momentum as the day progresses. One patient ornithologist estimated that the Red-eyed Vireo sings its memorable phrase—*look up, way up, tree top, see me, here-I-am!*—10,000 to 20,000 times a day!

Visual identification of the Red-eyed Vireo is difficult, because its olive-brown color conceals it well among the foliage of deciduous trees. Although this vireo does indeed have red eyes, that feature can only be seen through powerful binoculars in excellent light conditions. Your best clue is to look for the white eyebrow and gray crown separated by a black line.

Similar Species: Warbling Vireo lacks the black line and the gray crown above the white eyebrow. Blue-headed Vireo (p. 103) has white 'spectacles.'

Quick I.D.: sparrow-sized; sexes similar; gray crown bordered by black; white eyebrow; green back; white underparts; red eyes.
Size: 6 in.

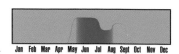

Jan Feb Mar Apr May Jun Jul Aug Sept Oct Nov Dec

Blue-winged Warbler
Vermivora pinus

breeding

As recently as the mid-1800s, the Blue-winged Warbler began to move eastward from its Midwestern home, finding new breeding territories in the overgrown fields and pastures of abandoned human settlements. Its eastern expansion brought it into contact with the Golden-winged Warbler, a bird with completely different looks but similar habitat requirements and breeding biology, and there has been an increasing incidence of interspecies breeding. The ranges of these two species overlap just outside Greater Boston, and there is a good chance you will see one of the two distinctive, fully fertile hybrids that are occasionally produced.

The Blue-winged Warbler and the Golden-winged Warbler do not breed in the Greater Boston area, but they can be seen in many of our deciduous woodland parks, especially during their spring migrations. An early morning stroll through Mt. Auburn Cemetery in May should produce an inspirational meeting with these lively, attractive birds.

Similar Species: Yellow Warbler (p. 106) lacks the black mask and the blue-gray wings. Golden-winged Warbler has a dark throat and white underparts. 'Brewster's Warbler' (hybrid) does not have as pure yellow underparts and might have bright yellow wing bars and a gray mantle. 'Lawrence's Warbler' (hybrid) has a black throat, a black mask and yellow underparts.

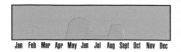

Jan Feb Mar Apr May Jun Jul Aug Sept Oct Nov Dec

Quick I.D.: smaller than a sparrow; yellow body; black eye line; blue-gray wings and tail; two light wing bars; dark legs. *Male:* brighter yellow on crown and nape. *Female:* yellow-green on head and nape; duller overall.
Size: 4–4³/₄ in.

Yellow Warbler

Dendroica petechia

The Yellow Warbler is common in willow trees, shrublands and brushy areas surrounding wetlands. From early May through August, this brilliantly colored warbler is easily found in appropriate habitats throughout our area. As a consequence of its abundance, it is usually the first warbler birdwatchers identify in their lives—and the first they see every spring thereafter.

Yellow Warblers migrate to the tropics for the winter, spending September to April in Mexico and South America. Following the first warm days of spring, the first Yellow Warblers return to our area, and their distinctive courtship song—*sweet-sweet-sweet I'm so-so sweet!*—is easily recognized despite the birds' eight-month absence. In true warbler fashion, the summertime activities of the Yellow Warbler are energetic and inquisitive: it flits from branch to branch in search of juicy caterpillars, aphids and beetles.

Similar Species: Wilson's Warbler has a small black cap. Blue-winged Warbler (p. 105) has a black eye line and a blue-gray tail and wings.

breeding

Quick I.D.: smaller than a sparrow; yellow overall; darker back, wings and tail; dark eyes and bill. *Male:* bold red streaking on breast. *Female:* breast is usually unstreaked. **Size:** 4–5 in.

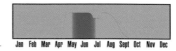

Jan Feb Mar Apr May Jun Jul Aug Sept Oct Nov Dec

Chestnut-sided Warbler

Dendroica pensylvanica

breeding

♂

Dropping down to human eye-level, the curious Chestnut-sided Warbler invites all into young deciduous stands with a hearty *so pleased pleased pleased to meet-cha!* greeting. This common woodland warbler appears genuinely hospitable, and in its flitty behavior it often passes within one branch of onlookers. The male's distinctive chestnut sides and white belly accentuate his brilliance and timeless style for springtime fashion.

Chestnut-sided Warblers are regular migrants in the Boston area, but they are found in far fewer numbers here than at higher-elevation woodlands to the west. Populations of this warbler have increased in Massachusetts in recent decades owing to the renewal of young forests. Prior to European colonization, the tall, continuous forests of Massachusetts would have provided habitat for the old-growth warblers rather than for the Chestnut-sided Warbler and similar birds that rely on young, brushy forests and clearings. It is now possible to see more Chestnut-sided Warblers in a single day than some of the great pioneering naturalists saw in their entire lives.

Similar Species: Male Bay-breasted Warbler lacks the white cheek and throat and has a dark cap. Male Cape May Warbler lacks the white underparts.

Jan Feb Mar Apr May Jun Jul Aug Sept Oct Nov Dec

Quick I.D.: smaller than a sparrow. *Breeding male:* white underparts; chestnut flanks; yellow crown; white cheek; light wing bars; black-and-green back. *Breeding female:* less intense markings and colors.
Size: 5 in.

Magnolia Warbler

Dendroica magnolia

The Magnolia Warbler is widely regarded as one of the most beautiful wood warblers in North America. Like a customized Cadillac, the Magnolia has all the luxury options—eyebrows, wing bars, a 'necklace,' a yellow rump and breast, tail patches and dark cheeks. As if aware of its stylish beauty, the Magnolia Warbler frequently seems to flaunt its colors to birdwatchers at close range. These beautiful warblers can be seen prancing in the low branches and shrubs as they refuel on newly emerged beetles, flies, wasps and caterpillars during migration.

Birdwatchers have many opportunities to see this glamorous warbler at Mt. Auburn Cemetery, Middlesex Fells Reservation, Nahant Thicket and Walden Pond during its spring migration. After a few short weeks in May, however, all Magnolias will have left our area in favor of cool, northerly spruce and fir forests.

Similar Species: Male Yellow-rumped Warbler (p. 109) has a yellow crown and lacks the yellow underparts. Male Cape May Warbler has a rufous cheek. Canada Warbler has solid blue-gray upperparts and yellow spectacles and lacks the yellow rump.

breeding

Quick I.D.: smaller than a sparrow.
Male: yellow underparts with bold, black streaks; black mask; white eyebrow; blue-gray crown; dark upperparts; white wing bars. *Female:* duller overall. *In flight:* yellow rump; white tail patches make a nearly complete band across dark tail.
Size: 4¹/₂–5 in.

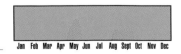

Jan Feb Mar Apr May Jun Jul Aug Sept Oct Nov Dec

Yellow-rumped Warbler

Dendroica coronata

breeding

This spirited songbird is as common as it is delightful. Its contrasting colors, curiosity and tinkling trill are enthusiastically admired by even the most jaded birdwatcher. The Yellow-rumped Warbler is the only warbler in the Boston area that can, uncommonly, be found during winter. It is not during the coldest months, however, that Yellow-rumps are most noticeable; rather it is from April to early May and again from September to early November that trees in parks and neighborhoods throughout the Boston area come alive with these colorful birds.

Most experienced birdwatchers call these birds 'Myrtle Warblers,' because they feed on myrtle berries in fall and winter. Until fairly recently, our white-throated form of the Yellow-rumped Warbler was considered a separate species from the western, yellow-throated form (called the 'Audubon's Warbler'). In recognition of the bird's eastern roots and distinct plumage, many birders remain defiant of the name change.

Similar Species: Magnolia Warbler (p. 108) has yellow underparts and white tail patches.

Jan Feb Mar Apr May Jun Jul Aug Sept Oct Nov Dec

Quick I.D.: smaller than a sparrow; blue-black back, tail and wings; yellow rump, shoulder patches and crown; white throat; faint white wing bars; dark breast band; white belly; dark cheek. *Male:* bright colors. *Female:* less intense colors.

Size: 5–6 in.

VIREOS & WARBLERS 109

Blackburnian Warbler

Dendroica fusca

In spring, the male Blackburnian Warbler is ablaze with a fiery orange throat. Regarded as one of North America's most beautiful warblers, Blackburnians joyfully are a fairly common migrant through the Boston area. Charging up through the Atlantic Flyway from their wintering grounds in the South American Andes, these brightly colored birds arrive in our area at about the second week in May.

At this time of year the migrating Blackburnians are joined by many other species of northward-moving warblers that ornament trees in Mt. Auburn Cemetery and other local woodlands like Christmas decorations. The Blackburnian's stay is short, however, and within a few weeks all the birds have moved on. Blackburnian Warblers offer a return engagement in September, but their fall wardrobe is so much more subdued than their spring attire that many birders choose to wait until next spring—a full year—to view them in their celebrated springtime splendor.

Similar Species: American Redstart (p. 113) has orange in its wings and tail, but not in its face or throat.

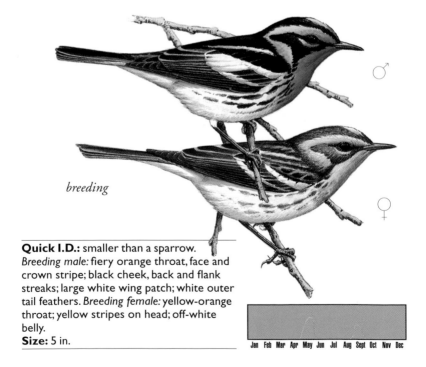

breeding

Quick I.D.: smaller than a sparrow.
Breeding male: fiery orange throat, face and crown stripe; black cheek, back and flank streaks; large white wing patch; white outer tail feathers. *Breeding female:* yellow-orange throat; yellow stripes on head; off-white belly.
Size: 5 in.

Jan Feb Mar Apr May Jun Jul Aug Sept Oct Nov Dec

Prairie Warbler

Dendroica discolor

breeding

Prairie Warblers are especially characteristic of the scrub oak and pitch pine barrens of southeastern Massachusetts. Elsewhere, densely overgrown fields filled with scattered shrubs and tree saplings, like those found in Middlesex Fells Reservation, make a good summer home for this fairly common warbler.

Prairie Warblers form loose breeding colonies—a reproductive strategy that is uncommon among warblers—which allows a single male to secure several mates and raise several families. One cost of a male's breeding success, however, is that he has to feed many more hungry mouths when all of the young have hatched. Male Prairie Warblers might return to the same prime breeding area for many years, until the vegetation becomes too tall and dense for their liking, but females usually move around—they seek out new mates annually.

Similar Species: Pine Warbler lacks the distinctive, dark streaking in the face and has lighter streaking on its sides. Immature and fall Bay-breasted Warbler and Blackpoll Warbler (p. 112) have white bellies and wing bars.

Quick I.D.: smaller than a sparrow. *Breeding male:* two dark streaks through face; streaked flanks; olive-yellow upper-parts; bright yellow face and underparts; inconspicuous chestnut streaks on back; two faint, yellowish wing bars; buffy-white undertail coverts. *Female:* duller. *Immature:* duller than female; grayish-olive streaking in face.

Size: 4³/₄ in.

Jan Feb Mar Apr May Jun Jul Aug Sept Oct Nov Dec

Blackpoll Warbler
Dendroica striata

Blackpolls, which weigh less than a wet teabag, are champion migrants among warblers. They pass through Massachusetts on their way between South America and their breeding grounds in northern Canada and Alaska. Unlike other warblers, which choose a landlocked migratory passage, Blackpolls shortcut their fall journey by flying south over the Atlantic Ocean, leaving land at Cape Cod and not landing again until they reach the coast of northern Venezuela.

During their spring migration, the bold breeding plumage of Blackpolls allows for easy identification. They pass through our area quite commonly at this time of year, but their activities are infrequently noticed because they generally fly at night and forage among the high treetops. When cold foggy weather and rains strike Boston in mid- to late May, Blackpoll Warblers are often grounded in Mt. Auburn Cemetery and other local 'migrant traps,' impatiently waiting in the trees for the weather to turn bright.

Similar Species: Black-and-white Warbler has dark legs and a striped, black-and-white crown. Black-capped Chickadee (p. 92) has dark legs and lacks the streaks on its flanks.

breeding

Quick I.D.: sparrow-sized; two white wing bars; orange legs. *Breeding male:* black cap and upperparts; white cheek; black-streaked underparts. *Breeding female:* streaked, greenish upperparts; black-streaked or white underparts; dirty cheek. *Fall adult:* greenish-gray, streaky crown, back and breast.
Size: 5¹/₂ in.

Jan Feb Mar Apr May Jun Jul Aug Sept Oct Nov Dec

American Redstart

Setophaga ruticilla

Like an over-energized wind-up toy, the American Redstart flits from branch to branch in a dizzying pursuit of prey. Even while it is perched, its tail gently waves or quickly flicks open and closed, flashing its colorful orange (male) or yellow (female) tail patches. This erratic and amusing behavior is easily observed on this bird's summering ground, as well as in its Central American wintering habitat, where it is affectionately known as *candelita* (little candle).

Although American Redstarts are one of the most common warblers to pass through the Boston area, their songs are so wonderfully varied that even after a full spring season, their songs can still linger as a confusing mystery. During the last two weeks of May and the first week of June, take a walk through one of our local woodlands to discover this bird's unique beauty, energy and enthusiasm.

Similar Species: Blackburnian Warbler (p. 110) has an orange throat and face and lacks the orange patches in the wings and tail. Red-winged Blackbird (p. 132) is much larger, with no red on its breast or tail.

Jan Feb Mar Apr May Jun Jul Aug Sept Oct Nov Dec

Quick I.D.: smaller than a sparrow.
Male: black overall; fiery orange patches in wings, tail and side of breast; white belly.
Female: olive-gray back; light underparts; peach yellow patches in wings, tail and shoulders.
Size: 5 in.

Ovenbird

Seiurus aurocapillus

The sharp, loud call of the Ovenbird rises forcefully each spring from the dense shrubs of Oxbow National Wildlife Refuge and Arnold Arboretum. The Ovenbird—or at least its song, *teacher teacher Teacher TEACHER*—is encountered frequently during Boston's refreshing spring mornings. This distinctive, familiar song announces the bird's presence in mature deciduous woods. The Ovenbird's noisy habit of walking through the dense undergrowth nearly reveals its precise location, but its cryptic plumage and refusal to become airborne frustrate many birders intent on a quick peek. Ovenbirds rarely expose themselves to the open forest; they seem most comfortable in the tangles of shrubs, stumps and dead leaves.

Efforts to protect and restore the integrity of our last remaining mature deciduous forests will ensure the continued presence and perpetuation of the Ovenbird in the Greater Boston community.

Similar Species: Hermit Thrush and Wood Thrush (p. 101) are much larger, and they lack the russet crown streak. Northern Waterthrush lacks the russet crown and has a white eyebrow.

Quick I.D.: sparrow-sized; sexes similar; heavily streaked breast; bold eye ring; olive-brown back; russet crown bordered by black; orange legs.
Size: 6 in.

Jan Feb Mar Apr May Jun Jul Aug Sept Oct Nov Dec

Common Yellowthroat
Geothlypis trichas

With so much diversity within North America's wood warbler family, it is no surprise that one species has forsaken forests in favor of cattail marshes. In our area, this energetic warbler reaches its highest abundance along wetland brambles and cattails, but it can also be seen and heard in the vegetation bordering many freshwater bodies or even in drier fields and second-growth thickets some distance from water. If you are keen on meeting a colorful, spirited yellowthroat, you should visit the edges of Nahant's dense thickets in late May, late August or early September.

The male Common Yellowthroat is easily identified by his black mask or by his oscillating *witchety-witchety-witchety!* song. Female yellowthroats are rarely seen. They quietly keep to their nests deep within the thick, low-growing vegetation. Yellowthroat chicks develop rapidly, and they soon leave the nest, allowing the parents to raise a second brood. Common Yellowthroat nests are often parasitized by Brown-headed Cowbirds.

Similar Species: Male is distinct. Nashville Warbler has dark brown legs and an eye ring. Female Wilson's Warbler has a yellow eyebrow and the hint of a dark cap.

Quick I.D.: smaller than a sparrow; orange legs; yellow throat and underparts; olive upperparts. *Male:* black mask with white border on forehead. *Female:* plain face (no mask).
Size: 4$^{1}/_{2}$–5$^{1}/_{2}$ in.

Jan Feb Mar Apr May Jun Jul Aug Sept Oct Nov Dec

Scarlet Tanager
Piranga olivacea

The tropical appearance of the male Scarlet Tanager's plumage reinforces the link between the forests of South America and those of eastern North America. A winter resident of the tropics and a breeder in Boston's mature deciduous woods, this tanager is vulnerable to deforestation at both extremes of its range.

Despite their blazing red plumage, Scarlet Tanagers can be difficult to see, mainly because they tend to stay high up in forest canopies. They sing a robin-like warble—*hurry-worry-lurry-scurry!*—that is frequently disregarded as coming from that more familiar woodland voice. Careful listeners will note that the song is shorter and burrier than a robin's, while novice birdwatchers can listen for the tanager's unique hiccup-like *chick-burr* call. If you are lucky, you might happen upon a tanager foraging close to the ground during rainy or foggy weather, particularly among the low foliage of Mt. Auburn Cemetery during May or September migration.

Similar Species: Northern Cardinal (p. 139) has a crest, a heavy bill and red wings. Male Baltimore Oriole (p. 136) is black and orange. Male Orchard Oriole is black and chestnut. Both male orioles have black heads. Female orioles have thinner bills and wing bars.

breeding

♂

Quick I.D.: larger than a sparrow.
Breeding male: unmistakable, magnificent scarlet body; black wings and tail.
Non-breeding male: yellow-green body; black wings and tail. *Female:* olive-yellow overall; no wing bars.
Size: 6¹/₂–7¹/₂ in.

Jan Feb Mar Apr May Jun Jul Aug Sept Oct Nov Dec

European Starling
Sturnus vulgaris

breeding

By 1920, 30 years after their intentional release in New York City's Central Park, European Starlings had firmly established themselves in Massachusetts. Within a decade, flocks of half a million birds were being reported. Today, European Starlings are one of the most common birds in Boston. Their presence is highlighted by astonishing numbers roosting communally under the Mystic River Bridge in Everett and under the Fore River Bridge in Quincy during the winter months. The total number of birds roosting in these two locations combined often exceeds 200,000!

Unfortunately, the expansion of starlings has come at the expense of many of our native birds, including the Purple Martin and the Eastern Bluebird, which are unable to defend their nest cavities against the aggressive starlings. If residents are unable to find joy in this bird's remarkable mimicry and astounding flocking behavior, they can take some comfort from the fact that starlings now provide a reliable and stable food source for a variety of woodland hawks and Merlins.

Similar Species: All blackbirds have longer tails and black bills. Purple Martin (p. 87) has a short bill.

Jan Feb Mar Apr May Jun Jul Aug Sept Oct Nov Dec

Quick I.D.: smaller than a robin; sexes similar; short tail. *Breeding:* dark, glossy plumage; long, yellow bill. *Non-breeding:* dark bill; spotty plumage. *Juvenile:* brown upperparts; gray-brown underparts; brown bill. **Size:** 8–9 in.

Gray Catbird
Dumetella carolinensis

The Gray Catbird is a sleek bird that commonly displays an unusual 'mooning' behavior—it raises its long, slender tail to show its chestnut undertail coverts. This behavior is one of the elements of courtship, and the coverts might help female catbirds choose the best mates.

The Gray Catbird is a bird of dense shrubs and thickets, and although it's relatively common in appropriate habitats, its distinctive call, rather than the bird itself, is what most people commonly encounter. During May and June, the Gray Catbird's unmistakable, cat-like 'meowing,' for which it is named, can be heard rising from shrubs at Nahant Thicket, Mt. Auburn Cemetery and the Boston Public Garden.

Similar Species: Northern Mockingbird (p.119) has white patches in its wings and tail.

Quick I.D.: smaller than a robin; sexes similar; slate gray body; black cap; chestnut undertail coverts; long, dark tail.
Size: 9 in.

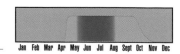

Jan Feb Mar Apr May Jun Jul Aug Sept Oct Nov Dec

Northern Mockingbird

Mimus polyglottos

In the early years of European colonization, the Northern Mockingbird was considered a rare and erratic summer resident throughout most of New England, but it is now a common year-round resident throughout much of our area. As agricultural and urban development blossomed, mockingbirds began to push northward into Massachusetts. Over time, with the help of consistently mild winter weather in our region since 1955, the creation of broken forest habitats and the planting of urban, fruit-bearing trees and shrubs, these fascinating birds have established themselves as a permanent fixture in our urban and rural communities.

The Northern Mockingbird is perhaps best known for its ability to mimic sounds. It will expertly imitate other birds, barking dogs and even musical instruments in its seeming quest to expand the size and diversity of its vocal repertoire. Scientific evidence suggests that mockingbirds with larger, more complex repertoires are better at attracting mates and intimidating nearby competitors.

Similar Species: Northern Shrike, seen only in winter months, has a black mask and a stout, hooked bill.

Jan Feb Mar Apr May Jun Jul Aug Sept Oct Nov Dec

Quick I.D.: robin-sized; sexes similar; white patches in black wings and tail; gray head and back; light underparts; long tail; thin bill.

Size: 10 in.

Cedar Waxwing
Bombycilla cedrorum

A faint, high-pitched, buzzy trill is often your first clue that waxwings are around. If you hear this sound, quickly scan the skies or neighborhood treetops to see these cinnamon-crested birds plying the skies in large flocks or darting out from tree limbs to snack on flying insects.

Cedar Waxwings are found in many habitats throughout Boston—wherever ripe berries provide abundant food supplies. They are most often seen in large flocks in late spring and fall, when they can quickly eat all the berries on fruit trees. Some people remember these visits not only for the birds' beauty, but because fermentation of the fruit occasionally renders the flock flightless from intoxication.

Similar Species: Tufted Titmouse (p. 93) lacks black face mask and lacks yellow on its belly.

Quick I.D.: smaller than a robin; sexes similar; fine, pale, silky-brown plumage; small crest; black mask; yellow belly wash; yellow-tipped tail; light undertail coverts; shiny red (waxy-looking) droplets on wing tips.
Size: 7–8 in.

Jan Feb Mar Apr May Jun Jul Aug Sept Oct Nov Dec

American Pipit

Anthus rubescens

American Pipits certainly earn their winter vacations—they breed in some of the harshest environments in North America. Once they return in fall from the arctic and alpine tundra of Labrador, Greenland and the arctic islands, pipits can be seen along shorelines and open areas throughout Greater Boston. Although the climate of their temporary surroundings might have changed, their disdain for trees and other tall forms of vegetation transcends their geographic relocation.

While visiting just about any open field or seashore during the migratory months, be sure to keep an eye open for the American Pipit. Like many shorebirds and blackbirds, the pipit forages almost exclusively in damp areas on the ground. The best way to identify this drab dresser is to watch its tail—if you are looking at an American Pipit, the tail will bob rhythmically.

Similar Species: Savannah Sparrow (p. 125) has a yellow lore and light legs, and it is stockier overall. Horned Lark has a black mask, a solid, dark 'necklace' and black 'horns.'

non-breeding

Jan Feb Mar Apr May Jun Jul Aug Sept Oct Nov Dec

Quick I.D.: sparrow-sized; sexes similar; bobs its tail; brown-gray upperparts; lightly streaked underparts; dark tail with white outer tail feathers; slim bill; black legs.
Size: 6¹/₂ in.

Eastern Towhee
Pipilo erythrophthalmus

This large, cocky sparrow is most often heard scratching away leaves and debris under dense shrubs and bushes long before it is seen. Among the deep shadows of shrubs, the Eastern Towhee's sharp *Drink your Teeea* positively identifies this secretive sparrow. To observe this bird, it is best to learn a few birding tricks—squeaking and pishing are irresistible sounds for towhees. Towhees will soon pop out from cover to investigate the curious noise, revealing their surprising combination of colors.

The Eastern Towhee is a summer resident in Boston-area renewed-growth forests, brambles and forest openings, such as those at Middlesex Fells Reservation and especially in the scrub oak and pitch pine forests of southeastern Massachusetts. It was formerly grouped together with the western Spotted Towhee as a single species: the Rufous-sided Towhee.

Similar Species: American Robin (p. 102) is larger and has no white on its breast. Dark-eyed Junco (p. 129) is smaller and has completely white outer tail feathers, rather than just white tail corners.

Quick I.D.: smaller than a robin; rufous-colored flanks; white outer tail corners; white underparts; red eyes. *Male:* black head, breast and upperparts. *Female:* brown head, breast and upperparts.
Size: 8–9 in.

Jan Feb Mar Apr May Jun Jul Aug Sept Oct Nov Dec

Chipping Sparrow

Spizella passerina

Hopping around freshly mowed lawns, the cheery Chipping Sparrow goes about its business unconcerned by the busy world of suburban Boston. One of Massachusetts's most widespread species, the Chipping Sparrow brings birdwatching to those who rarely venture from their homes—these sparrows frequently nest in our backyards, building their small nest cups with dried vegetation and lining them with animal hair.

Chipping Sparrows are delightful neighbors in our backyards, and they demand nothing more than a little privacy around an ornamental conifer where they have chosen to nest. They usually attempt to raise two broods every year in Boston—they lay three or four small, greenish-blue eggs in mid-May and later near the beginning of July, should conditions prove favorable.

Similar Species: American Tree Sparrow is only a winter resident and has a black central breast spot. Field Sparrow (p. 124) has a pink bill and a gray eyebrow.

breeding

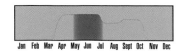

Jan Feb Mar Apr May Jun Jul Aug Sept Oct Nov Dec

Quick I.D.: small sparrow; sexes similar; red crown; white eyebrow; black eye line; clear, whitish-gray breast; streaked back.
Size: 5¹/₂ in.

Field Sparrow

Spizella pusilla

The innocent, unmarked face of the Field Sparrow gives this common bird a perpetual look of adolescence. Like a teenage boy prior to his first shave, the Field Sparrow has a soft, wholesome look, highlighted by its pink bill and untainted eye.

Many sparrows have very descriptive and accurate names, but the Field Sparrow's name is somewhat misleading. An inhabitant of overgrown meadows and bushy areas—which seem to be decreasing in our area—the Field Sparrow tends to avoid open, expansive, grassy fields. These birds have adapted well to the shrubby growth in clearings below power lines.

Field Sparrows often nest far away from human developments, but not far enough from Brown-headed Cowbirds, which can parasitize more than one-quarter of the nests in our area, affecting this sparrow's reproductive success. So far, cowbirds have not significantly decreased the population of these tireless singers, who offer their voices on hot summer days when most other singers are quiet.

Similar Species: Chipping Sparrow (p. 123) has a white eyebrow and a black eye line. American Tree Sparrow has a dark breast spot and a dark bill.

Quick I.D.: mid-sized sparrow; sexes similar; reddish crown; plain gray underparts; pink bill; light gray eyebrow; rusty brown back.
Size: 5–6 in.

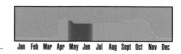

Jan Feb Mar Apr May Jun Jul Aug Sept Oct Nov Dec

Savannah Sparrow

Passerculus sandwichensis

The Savannah Sparrow is a common bird of the open country. In Massachusetts, it prefers to breed in open moorlands, fields of weedy annuals and grasses and along sand dunes on the coast. There are relatively few breeding records for Savannah Sparrows in the Boston area, with most birds choosing the grassy fields adjacent to Logan International Airport. The 'Ipswich Sparrow,' a subspecies of the Savannah that breeds only on Sable Island, Nova Scotia, can be found wintering along Boston-area beaches, such as those in Squantum.

When escaping danger, the Savannah Sparrow resorts to flight only as a last alternative—it prefers to run swiftly and inconspicuously through long grass—and it is most often seen darting across roads and open fields. Its dull brown plumage and streaked breast conceal it perfectly in the grasses of its favorite habitat. The Savannah Sparrow's distinctive buzzy song—*tea-tea-tea-teeea today*—and the yellow patch in front of its eye are the best ways to distinguish it from the other Boston-area sparrows.

Similar Species: Song Sparrow (p. 127) has a prominent breast spot and no yellow on the face.

'Ipswich Sparrow'

Jan Feb Mar Apr May Jun Jul Aug Sept Oct Nov Dec

Quick I.D.: mid-sized sparrow; sexes similar; streaked underparts and upperparts; mottled brown above; dark cheek; many have yellow lore.
Size: 5–6 in.

Saltmarsh Sharp-tailed Sparrow

Ammodramus caudacutus

Differentiating between all those little brown birds known as sparrows can seem like a nightmarish challenge. With the Saltmarsh Sharp-tailed Sparrow, however, all you have to do is look it in the eye to see the unique orange facial triangle that encompasses its gray ear patch and eye. Its streaky, buff-colored breast and sides also separate it from many other sparrows. A third clue to this sparrow's identity is its choice of habitat: the tidal salt marshes of eastern Massachusetts.

Unlike other sparrow species, breeding Saltmarsh Sharp-tails do not form pair bonds. Males do not defend a breeding territory or help the females raise the young. Instead, a male flies through the marsh, occasionally stopping to attract a mate through song. After mating, the male moves on to search for other potential mates, while the female begins the business of raising the young or looking for another mate herself.

Similar Species: Field Sparrow (p. 124), winter American Tree Sparrow and Seaside Sparrow all lack the orange facial triangle. Nelson's Sharp-tailed Sparrow has much lighter streaking on its breast, flanks and back, and it is only in the Boston area briefly during migration.

Quick I.D.: small sparrow; sexes similar; buffy breast and flanks streaked with brown; gray ear patch surrounded by orange triangle; gray central crown stripe; unstreaked gray nape.
Size: 5¹/₄ in.

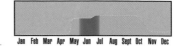

Jan Feb Mar Apr May Jun Jul Aug Sept Oct Nov Dec

Song Sparrow
Melospiza melodia

The Song Sparrow's drab, heavily streaked plumage doesn't prepare you for its symphonic song, which stands among the best in the Boston area for complexity and rhythm. This commonly heard bird is one of the first in song during spring, and it seems to bear good news by singing *hip-hip-hip hooray boys, the spring is here again.*

This year-round resident is easily found in a wide variety of habitats: marshes, thickets, brambles, weedy fields and woodland edges. Some birds withdraw during winter, but many continue to be encountered at backyard feeders and parks around the city.

Song Sparrows are most easily identified by their grayish facial streaks while they are perched. Flying birds often characteristically pump their tails.

Similar Species: Fox Sparrow is very heavily streaked and has a different song. Savannah Sparrow (p. 125) has a yellow lore. Lincoln's Sparrow has a buffy wash across the breast.

Jan Feb Mar Apr May Jun Jul Aug Sept Oct Nov Dec

Quick I.D.: large sparrow; sexes similar; heavy breast streaks form central spot; brown plumage; striped head.

Size: 6–7 in.

White-throated Sparrow

Zonotrichia albicollis

The catchy song of the White-throated Sparrow is often on the lips of weekend cottagers returning from the wooded wilds. By whistling the distinctive *Old Sam Peabody Peabody Peabody* to themselves, people bring some of the atmosphere of the woods home to the city. This voice of conifer forests is a sure sign of summer in the cottage country of western Massachusetts. The White-throat's striped head and white throat allow it to stand out from House Finches and bland sparrow relatives.

In late April, early May and October, thousands of White-throated Sparrows pass through Boston. Many of them stop at Mt. Auburn Cemetery or the Boston Public Garden to take a breather and catch a quick meal. During winter, too, many of these birds remain in town to forage for plant seeds or to munch on birdfeeder offerings in our parks and backyards.

Similar Species: White-crowned Sparrow has a less conspicuous whitish throat and a pink bill.

Quick I.D.: large sparrow; sexes similar; black and white or black and tan stripes on head; white throat; unstreaked, light gray breast; yellow lore; rusty brown upperparts.
Size: 6¹/₂–7 in.

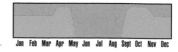

Jan Feb Mar Apr May Jun Jul Aug Sept Oct Nov Dec

Dark-eyed Junco

Junco hyemalis

Dark-eyed Juncos are abundant winter visitors throughout the Boston area. They are ground dwellers, and they are frequently seen flushing from the undergrowth along wooded park trails. Their distinctive, white outer tail feathers flash in alarm as they fly down a narrow, open path before disappearing into a concealing thicket.

Just before departing for their northern breeding grounds in early April, Dark-eyed Juncos sing their musical trills, which are easily confused with those of the Chipping Sparrow. The junco's distinctive smacking call and its habit of double-scratching at forest litter also help identify it. Juncos are frequent guests at birdfeeders throughout Boston, usually preferring to clean up the scraps that have fallen to the ground.

Similar Species: Eastern Towhee (p. 122) is larger and has conspicuous rufous sides. Male Brown-headed Cowbird (p. 135) lacks the white outer tail feathers and the white belly.

Jan Feb Mar Apr May Jun Jul Aug Sept Oct Nov Dec

Quick I.D.: mid-sized sparrow; sexes similar (female is somewhat duller); slate gray head and upperparts; white belly; light-colored bill; white outer tail feathers.
Size: 5–6 1/2 in.

Snow Bunting
Plectrophenax nivalis

♂

♀

non-breeding

When late fall snows dust the
fields and roadsides of the greater Boston
area, Snow Buntings are surely close behind.
Unlike most migrant songbirds found along the Eastern
Seaboard, Snow Buntings remain for the winter in small, tight flocks.
Although wintering Snow Buntings prefer the endless and expansive open
areas of the northern Great Plains, each winter a few of these hardy
songbirds arrive in Boston to scratch and peck at exposed seeds and grains
in open areas.

Built with longer bones in their feet than most other perching birds, Snow
Buntings are predominantly ground-dwellers that shun the lofty perches of
trees and shrubs. As flocks of Snow Buntings lift in unison, the startling
white, black and tan contrast of their plumage flashes characteristically
against the clean, white backdrop.

Similar Species: Lapland Longspur has a brown-mottled back and
doesn't show the white, black and tan contrast in flight.

Quick I.D.: large sparrow; sexes similar.
Non-breeding: white underparts; light,
golden-brown crown and back (less on
back in male); pale bill. *Breeding:* black and
white plumage (some gray or brown in
female). *In flight:* black wing tips, tail and
back contrast with light plumage.
Size: 6–7¹/₂ in.

Jan Feb Mar Apr May Jun Jul Aug Sept Oct Nov Dec

Bobolink
Dolichonyx oryzivorus

♂

♀

breeding

In spring, small flocks of Bobolinks return to weedy fields in the Greater Boston area to grace cool mornings with their songs. The males, which look as though they're wearing tuxedos backwards, arrive a few days before the females and perform their bubbly, tinkly song—*bob-o-link bob-o-link, spink, spank, spink*—assuring farmers and naturalists that spring is here.

At first glimpse, Bobolinks look every bit a sparrow, especially the drab females, which lack the males' style for fashion. These birds are not sparrows, however, but blackbirds. This kinship is evident in their polygynous breeding strategy, and males that acquire prime hayfields can mate and defend several nesting females.

The fall migration of Bobolinks is a spectacular sight. Flocks leaving the northern coast congregate with others from the west, soon numbering in the thousands. These flocks descend on rice crops in the southeast states to feed, and they were given the name 'rice birds' for their costly appetites. Bobolinks winter in rice fields in South America.

Similar Species: Brown-headed Cowbird (p. 135) has a black back. Sparrows tend to lack the pointy tail feathers.

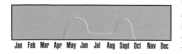

Jan Feb Mar Apr May Jun Jul Aug Sept Oct Nov Dec

Quick I.D.: large sparrow–sized; pointed tail feathers. *Breeding male:* black head and body; buffy nape; white rump and shoulders. *Female* and *Non-breeding male:* buffy brown body; dark crown streaks; dark eye line.
Size: 6–8 in.

Red-winged Blackbird

Agelaius phoeniceus

From March through July, no Boston marsh is free from the loud calls and bossy, aggressive nature of the Red-winged Blackbird. A springtime walk around Great Meadows National Wildlife Refuge or through the brush at any wetland or field will be accompanied by this bird's loud, raspy and persistent *konk-a-reee* or *eat my CHEEEzies* song.

♂

♀

The male's bright red shoulders (called 'epaulettes') are his most important tool in the strategic and intricate displays he uses to defend his territory from rivals and to attract a mate. In experiments, males whose red shoulders were painted black soon lost their territories to rivals they had previously defeated. The female's interest lies not in the individual combatants, however, but in the nesting habitat, and a male who can successfully defend a large area of dense cattails will breed with many females. After the females have built their concealed nests and laid their eggs, the male continues his persistent vigil.

Similar Species: Common Grackle (p. 134) and Brown-headed Cowbird (p. 135) both lack the red shoulder patches.

Quick I.D.: smaller than a robin. *Male:* all-black plumage; large red patch bordered by creamy yellow on each shoulder.
Female: brown overall; heavily streaked; hint of red on shoulder.
Size: 7^1/$_2$–9^1/$_2$ in.

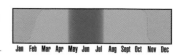

Jan Feb Mar Apr May Jun Jul Aug Sept Oct Nov Dec

Eastern Meadowlark
Sturnella magna

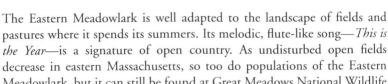

The Eastern Meadowlark is well adapted to the landscape of fields and pastures where it spends its summers. Its melodic, flute-like song—*This is the Year*—is a signature of open country. As undisturbed open fields decrease in eastern Massachusetts, so too do populations of the Eastern Meadowlark, but it can still be found at Great Meadows National Wildlife Refuge and Logan International Airport.

Eastern Meadowlarks are both showy and perfectly camouflaged. Their yellow sweater with the black V-neck and their white outer tail feathers serve to attract mates. Courting meadowlarks face one another, raise their bills high and perform a grassy field ballet. Oddly, the colorful breast and white tail feathers are also used to attract the attention of potential predators. Foxes, hawks or falcons focus on these bold features in pursuit, but then their prey mysteriously disappears into the grass whenever the meadowlark chooses to turn its back or fold away its white tail flags.

Similar Species: None.

breeding

Jan Feb Mar Apr May Jun Jul Aug Sept Oct Nov Dec

Quick I.D.: robin-sized; sexes similar; mottled brown upperparts; black V on breast; yellow throat and belly; white outer tail feathers; striped head.
Size: 8–10 in.

Common Grackle

Quiscalus quiscula

The Common Grackle is a noisy bird that prefers to feed on the ground in open areas. Birdfeeders in rural areas can attract large numbers of these blackish birds, whose cranky disposition drives away most other birds. The Common Grackle is easily identified by its long tail, large bill and dark plumage, which can shine with hues of green, purple, blue and bronze in bright light.

The Common Grackle is a poor but spirited singer. Usually while perched in a shrub, a male grackle will slowly take a deep breath that inflates his breast and causes his feathers to rise; then he closes his eyes and gives out a loud, surprising *swaaaack*, not unlike a rusty gate. Despite our perception of the Common Grackle's musical weakness, following his 'song,' the male smugly and proudly poses with his bill held high.

Similar Species: Red-winged Blackbird (p. 132) and Brown-headed Cowbird (p. 135) have relatively shorter bills and tails and have dark eyes. American Crow (p. 91) is much larger and bulkier. Rusty Blackbird in fall plumage has a rusty tinge on its head, back and wings, and spring and summer birds are all black and generally lack the multi-colored iridescence.

Quick I.D.: jay-sized; sexes similar; glossy black plumage with purple and bronze iridescence; long tail; yellow eyes; large bill.
Size: 11–13 in.

Brown-headed Cowbird

Molothrus ater

Since it first arrived in Massachusetts in the late 1800s, the Brown-headed Cowbird has firmly established itself within the matrix of our region's bird life. This gregarious bird is very common in outlying agricultural areas, and it can be seen just about anywhere.

Female cowbirds do not incubate their own eggs; instead they lay them in the nests of many songbirds. Cowbird eggs have a short incubation period, and the cowbird chicks often hatch before the host songbird's own chicks. Many songbirds will continue to feed the fast-growing cowbird chick even after it has outgrown its surrogate parent. In its efforts to get as much food as possible, a cowbird chick might squeeze the host's own young out of the nest. The populations of some songbirds have been reduced in part by the activities of the Brown-headed Cowbird, but other songbird species recognize the foreign egg, and they either eject it from their nest or they build a new nest.

Similar Species: Common Grackle (p. 134) and Rusty Blackbird have yellow eyes. Female Red-winged Blackbird (p. 132) has much more streaking on its underparts.

♀

♂

Jan Feb Mar Apr May Jun Jul Aug Sept Oct Nov Dec

Quick I.D.: smaller than a robin; dark eyes. *Male:* metallic-looking, glossy black plumage; soft brown head. *Female:* brownish gray overall; slight breast streaks.
Size: 6–8 in.

Baltimore Oriole
Icterus galbula

Although it is a common summer resident of city parks and woodlands, the Baltimore Oriole is seldom seen. Unlike the American Robin, which inhabits the human domain of shrubs and lawns, the Baltimore Oriole nests and feeds in the tallest deciduous trees available. This bird's hanging, six-inch-deep, pouch-like nest is deceptively strong, and a vacant nest, which is easily seen on bare trees in fall, is often the only indication that a pair of orioles summered in an area.

From mid-May to mid-June, the park-like college campuses for which Boston is famous are among the most productive destinations for oriole-starved Boston-area birdwatchers. The male Baltimore Oriole's striking, Halloween-like, black-and-orange plumage flashes like embers amidst the dense foliage of the treetops, while his slow, purposeful *Peter Peter here here Peter Peter* song drips down to eager listeners along the forest floor.

Similar Species: Orchard Oriole is smaller and has chestnut, rather than orange, plumage.

Quick I.D.: smaller than a robin.
Male: brilliant orange belly, flanks, outer tail feathers and rump; black hood, wings and tail. *Female:* gray-green upperparts; orangish underparts; some have a faint hood.
Size: 7–8 in.

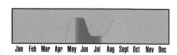

Jan Feb Mar Apr May Jun Jul Aug Sept Oct Nov Dec

House Finch
Carpodacus mexicanus

♂

♀

The House Finch is one of the earliest voices to announce the coming of spring. These common city and country birds sing their melodies from backyards, parks, ivy vines and telephone lines.

During the 1920s and '30s, this bird, which is native to the American Southwest, was a popular cage bird, and it was sold across the continent as the 'Hollywood Finch.' Illegal releases of the cage birds resulted in a wild population on Long Island in the 1940s, and they spread through eastern Massachusetts in the 1960s and '70s. The increase of House Finches has recently been reversed, however, as they have become vulnerable to disease. Birds with bald patches or crusty eyes, seen at backyard feeders, often indicate the presence of this disease.

Similar Species: Male Purple Finch is raspberry-colored and has unstreaked undertail coverts, and the female has a brown cheek contrasting with a white eyebrow and a mustache stripe.

Quick I.D.: sparrow-sized. *Male:* deep red forehead, eyebrow and throat; buffy gray belly; brown cheek; streaked sides and undertail coverts. *Female:* brown overall; streaked underparts; lacks prominent eyebrow.
Size: 5–6 in.

Jan Feb Mar Apr May Jun Jul Aug Sept Oct Nov Dec

American Goldfinch
Carduelis tristis

♀

♂

breeding

In spring, the American Goldfinch swings over fields in its distinctive, undulating flight, and it fills the air with its jubilant *po-ta-to chip* call. This bright, cheery songbird is commonly seen during summer in weedy fields, roadsides and backyards, where it often feeds on thistle seeds. The American Goldfinch delays nesting until July, August and even September to ensure a dependable source of insects, thistles and dandelion seeds to feed its young.

The American Goldfinch is a common backyard bird in parts of the Boston area, and it is attracted to feeding stations that offer a supply of niger (or 'thistle') seed. Unfortunately, goldfinches are easily bullied at feeders by larger sparrows and finches. Only goldfinches and Pine Siskins invert for food, however, so a special finch feeder with openings below the perches is ideal for ensuring a steady stream of what some people call 'wild canaries.'

Similar Species: Yellow Warbler (p. 106) does not have black on its forehead or wings. Evening Grosbeak is much larger and has broad, white wing patches.

Quick I.D.: smaller than a sparrow. *Breeding male:* black forehead, wings and tail; canary-yellow body; wings show white in flight. *Female* and *Non-breeding male:* no black on forehead; yellow-green overall; black wings and tail.
Size: 4¹/₂–5¹/₂ in.

Jan Feb Mar Apr May Jun Jul Aug Sept Oct Nov Dec

Northern Cardinal
Cardinalis cardinalis

Never far apart, male and female cardinals softly vocalize to one another year-round, not just through the breeding season. Their ritualized, beak-to-beak feeding reinforces the romantic appeal and bond of these easily identified birds. Although the regal male does little more than warble to the female while she constructs the nest, his parental duties will soon keep him busy. After the eggs have hatched, the nestlings and the brooding female will remain in the nest while the male provides much of the food for the entire family.

The Northern Cardinal is becoming more common at Boston's backyard feeders, having steadily expanded its range from the south, and many homeowners vividly remember the day their yards were first graced by its presence. As if grateful to residents with feeders, Northern Cardinals offer up their bubbly *What cheer! What cheer! Birdie-birdie-birdie What cheer!* to awaken Boston neighborhoods.

Similar Species: Male Scarlet Tanager (p. 116) has a black tail and wings and no crest.

Quick I.D.: smaller than a robin.
Male: unmistakable; red overall; black mask and throat; pointed crest; red, conical bill.
Female: considerably duller plumage.
Immature: like a female, but with a dark bill.
Size: 8–9 in.

Jan Feb Mar Apr May Jun Jul Aug Sept Oct Nov Dec

Rose-breasted Grosbeak
Pheucticus ludovicianus

The male Rose-breasted Grosbeak has a voice to match his magnificent plumage, and he flaunts both in treetop performances. Although the female lacks the formal dress of her mate, she shares his musical talents—whether the nest is incubated by the male or the female, the developing young are continually introduced into the world of song by the brooding parent.

This common songster's boldness does not go unnoticed by the appreciative birding community, which eagerly anticipates the male's annual spring concert in Mt. Auburn Cemetery and the Blue Hills Reservation. Boston birders keen on observing this bird's nesting behavior should be able to find a pair at Willowdale State Forest in Ipswich or Oxbow National Wildlife Refuge.

The Rose-breasted Grosbeak is one of the few songbirds in which the male does not acquire his full plumage until his second breeding season. First-year males are brown where adults are black, and they usually have less rose color.

Similar Species: Male is distinctive. Female Purple Finch and sparrows are generally smaller.

Quick I.D.: smaller than a robin; light-colored, conical bill. *Male:* black hood; rose breast; black back and wings; white rump; white wing bars. *Female:* heavily streaked with brown; white eyebrow; light throat.
Size: 7–8 in.

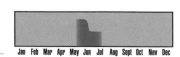

Jan Feb Mar Apr May Jun Jul Aug Sept Oct Nov Dec

Indigo Bunting
Passerina cyanea

Metallic-blue male Indigo Buntings are frequently encountered in open areas of overgrown fields and along forest edges. Perched atop a shrub or thicket, the males conduct elaborate tactical maneuvers with song. With rival males only a voice away, Indigo Buntings call continuously through the day, attempting to maintain superiority over their peers. Neighboring males copy and learn from one another, producing 'song territories.' Each male in a song territory adds a personal variation to the basic tune of *fire-fire, where-where, here-here, see-it see-it.*

Indigo Buntings are widespread throughout our area during summer, popping out of dense bushes anywhere from the Taunton River in Middleboro to Willowdale State Forest in Ipswich. They build a small cup nest low to the ground in an upright crotch among a shrubby tangle. Once their nesting duties are complete, these buntings are quick to leave our area, beginning their exodus in early September after a partial molt.

Similar Species: Eastern Bluebird (p. 99) is larger and has a red breast and a slimmer body. Female Indigo Bunting is similar to many sparrows, but sparrows usually have more heavily streaked plumage.

Quick I.D.: sparrow-sized; conical bill. *Male:* turquoise blue plumage; darker wings and tail. *Female:* soft brown overall; hints of blue on rump.
Size: 5¹/₂ in.

Jan Feb Mar Apr May Jun Jul Aug Sept Oct Nov Dec

House Sparrow
Passer domesticus

This common backyard bird often confuses novice birdwatchers because the females and immatures can be very nondescript. The male is relatively conspicuous—he has a black bib, a gray cap and white lines trailing down from his mouth (as though he has spilled milk on himself)—and he sings a continuous, monotone series of *cheep-cheep-cheep* notes. The best field mark for the female, however, apart from her pale eyebrows, is that there are no distinctive field marks.

The House Sparrow was introduced to North America in the 1850s to control insects. The majority of its diet is seeds, however, and it has become somewhat of a pest. The House Sparrow's aggressive nature usurps several native songbirds from nesting cavities, and its boldness often drives other birds away from backyard feeders. The House Sparrow and the European Starling, two of the most common birds in Boston and outlying farms, are a constant reminder of the negative impact of human introductions on natural systems.

Similar Species: Male is distinctive. Female is similar to female sparrows and finches, but she tends to lack any distinctive markings whatsoever.

Quick I.D.: mid-sized sparrow; brownish-gray belly. *Male:* black throat; gray forehead; white jowl; chestnut nape. *Female:* plain; unstreaked; pale eyebrow; mottled back and wings.
Size: 5¹/₂–6¹/₂ in.

Jan Feb Mar Apr May Jun Jul Aug Sept Oct Nov Dec

Watching Birds

Identifying your first new bird can be so satisfying that you just might become addicted to birdwatching. Luckily, birdwatching does not have to be expensive. It all hinges on how involved in this hobby you want to get. Setting up a simple backyard feeder is an easy way to get to know the birds sharing your neighborhood, and some people simply find birdwatching a pleasant way to complement a nightly walk with the dog or a morning commute into work.

Many people enjoy going to urban parks and feeding the wild birds that have become accustomed to humans. This activity provides people with intimate contact with urban-dwelling birds, but remember that birdseed, or better yet the birds' natural food items, are much healthier for the birds than bread and crackers.

SEASONS OF BIRDWATCHING

Spring

Spring is a welcomed sight for birders, many of whom will be enthusiastically seeking out early migrants at the first sign of warm weather. The early appearance of the Horned Lark, Red-winged Blackbird and American Robin is a reliable indication that spring is just around the corner. As soon as inland water is free from ice, great concentrations of waterfowl can be found wading through flooded fields and the swollen floodplains of local rivers. During March, sea ducks, loons and grebes are commonly found along local bays and harbors, and in mid-April uncountable flocks of shorebirds, gulls and terns are descending along our shorelines after a long journey from distant wintering grounds. For a brief period, local parks and backyards are alive with the bustling activity of migrant land birds. Thousands of sparrows pass through our city each spring, and by early to mid-May, most of the tiny wood warblers have arrived. Sporting their brightest colors, species such as the Blackburnian Warbler and Scarlet Tanager are a delight to see. By the end of the month, many birds have departed for their northern breeding grounds and our city's woodlands, bays and marshes have come to a migratory stand-still; it is time for the serious business of nesting.

Summer

Songs are silenced as daytime temperatures rise and the task of breeding gets underway. Although many of our warblers and sparrows are migratory, summers in the Boston area still offer many sights for the avid birdwatcher. The mixed woods of the Willowdale State Forest host such nesting species as the Yellow Warbler and Scarlet Tanager, while Marsh Wrens and Saltmarsh Sharp-tailed Sparrows can be found nesting among the tall grasses and cattails of Belle Isle Marsh Reservation. By July and August, many shorebirds are once again retreating south, signaling that the fall birding season will soon be upon us.

Fall

Fall migration is a prolonged affair, beginning as early as July and extending well into December. In early July, post-breeding shorebirds are once again gathering along local beaches and tidal pools. The annual hawk migration—an anticipated event for many—is at its peak during the second and third weeks of September, when thousands of individuals, including the Broad-winged Hawk and Sharp-shinned Hawk, can be seen in a single day. September is also the time to watch for migrating land birds and rarities—warblers, swallows, vireos and flycatchers are at a period of greatest abundance, gracing our skies and swarming parks and beaches. Sparrow and kinglet migrations commence in mid-September, followed by a mass movement of waterfowl. During the fall season, many of the warblers, ducks, gulls and shorebirds have acquired frustratingly similar plumages, but this season has its own benefits: this period of movement is less concentrated than in spring, providing a longer time frame for observing birds.

Winter

Open water and relatively mild winters attract thousands of waterbirds to the Massachusetts coast. Winter residents are plentiful and predictable: along Outer Boston Harbor and Newburyport, expect to see Common Loons, Red-necked Grebes, Great Cormorants and Purple Sandpipers. Some years bring rarities, such as the Pacific Loon, and it can be certain that the Massachusetts coast is well patrolled by birders to spot any such occurrence. Boston harbor hosts rafts of wintering waterfowl, including thousands of Greater Scaup and Common Eiders. Meanwhile, inland, backyard feeders are visited regularly by jays, chickadees and finches.

BIRDING OPTICS

Most people who are interested in birdwatching will eventually buy a pair of binoculars. They help you identify key bird characteristics, such as plumage and bill color, and they also help you identify other birders! Birdwatchers are a friendly sort, and a chat among birders is all part of the experience.

You'll use your binoculars often, so select a pair that will contribute to the quality of your birdwatching experience—they don't have to be expensive. If you need help deciding which pair is right for you, talk to other birdwatchers or to someone at your local nature center. Many models are available, and when shopping for binoculars it's important to keep two things in mind: weight and magnification.

One of the first things you'll notice about binoculars (apart from the price extremes) is that they all have two numbers associated with them (8 x 40, for example). The first number, which is always the smallest, is the magnification (how large the bird will appear); the second number is the size (in millimeters) of the objective lens (the larger end). It might seem important at first to get the highest magnification possible, but a reasonable magnification of 7x to 8x is optimal for all-purpose birding, because it draws you fairly close to most birds without causing too much vibration. Some shaking happens to everyone; to overcome it, rest the binoculars against a support, such as a partner's shoulder or a tree.

The size of the objective lens is really a question of birding conditions and weight. Because wider lenses (40–50 mm) will bring in more light, they are preferred for birding in low-light situations (like before sunrise or after sunset). If these aren't the conditions that you will be pursuing, a light pair that has an objective lens diameter of less than 30 mm could be the right choice. Because binoculars tend to feel heavy after hanging around your neck all day, the compact models are becoming increasingly popular. If you have a pair that is heavy, you can purchase a strap that redistributes part of the weight to the shoulders and lower back.

Another valuable piece of equipment is a spotting scope. It is very useful when you are trying to sight waterfowl, shorebirds or soaring raptors, but it is really of no use if you are intent on seeing forest birds. A good spotting scope has a magnification of about 40x. It has a sturdy tripod or a window mount for the car. Be wary of second-hand models of telescopes that are designed for seeing stars. Their magnification is too great for birdwatching.

One of the advantages of having a scope is that you will be able to see far-off birds, which can help during winter (to see waterfowl overwintering offshore, for example) or during migration (to see shorebirds and raptors). By setting up in one spot (or by not even leaving your car) you can observe faraway flocks that would be little more than specks in your binoculars.

With these simple pieces of equipment (none of which is truly essential) and this handy field guide, anyone can enjoy birds in their area. After experiencing the thrill of a couple of hard-won identifications, you will find yourself taking your binoculars on walks, drives and trips to the beach and cabin. As rewards accumulate with experience, you might find the books and photos piling up and your trips being planned just to see birds!

BIRDING BY EAR

Sometimes, bird listening can be more effective than bird watching. Many birds are difficult to see because they stay hidden in treetops, but you can learn to identify them by their songs. The technique of birding by ear is gaining popularity, because listening for birds can be more efficient, productive and rewarding than waiting for a visual confirmation. Birds have distinctive songs that they use to resolve territorial disputes, and sound is therefore a useful way to identify species. It is particularly useful when trying to watch some of the smaller forest-dwelling birds. Their size and often indistinct plumage can make a visual search of the forest canopy frustrating. To facilitate auditory searches, catchy paraphrases are included in the descriptions of many of the birds. If the paraphrase just doesn't seem to work for you (they are often a personal thing) be creative and try to find one that fits. By spending time playing the song over in your head, fitting words to it, the voices of birds soon become as familiar as the voices of family members. Many excellent CDs and tapes are available at bookstores and wild-bird stores for the songs of the birds in your area.

BIRDFEEDERS

They're messy, they can be costly, and they're sprouting up in neighborhoods everywhere. Feeding birds has become a common pastime in residential communities all over North America. Although the concept is fairly straightforward, as with anything else involving birds, feeders can become quite elaborate.

The great advantage to feeding birds is that neighborhood chickadees, jays, juncos and finches are enticed into regular visits. Don't expect birds to arrive at your feeder as soon as you set it up; it may take weeks for a few regulars to incorporate your yard into their daily routine. As the popularity of your feeder grows, the number of visiting birds will increase and more species will arrive. You will notice that your feeder is busier during the winter months, when natural foods are less abundant. You can increase the odds of a good avian turnout by using a variety of feeders and seeds. When a number of birds habitually visit your yard, maintaining the feeder becomes a responsibility, because the birds may begin to rely on it as a regular food source.

Larger birds tend to enjoy feeding on platforms or on the ground; smaller birds are comfortable on hanging seed dispensers. Certain seeds tend to attract specific birds; nature centers and wild-bird supply stores are the best places to ask how to attract a favorite species. It's mainly seed eaters that are attracted to backyards; some birds have no interest in feeders. Only the most committed birdwatcher will try to attract birds that are insect eaters, berry eaters or, in some extreme cases, scavengers!

The location of the feeder can influence the amount of business it receives from the neighborhood birds. Because birds are wild, they are instinctively wary, and they are unlikely to visit an area where they might come under attack. When putting up your feeder, think like a bird. A good, clear view with convenient escape routes is always appreciated. Cats like birdfeeders that are close to the ground and within pouncing distance from a bush; obviously, birds don't. Above all, a birdfeeder should be in view of a favorite window, where you can sit and enjoy the rewarding interaction of your appreciative feathered guests.

Glossary

accipiter: a forest hawk (genus *Accipiter*); characterized by a long tail and short, rounded wings; feeds mostly on birds.

brood: *n.* a family of young from one hatching; *v.* sit on eggs so as to hatch them.

conifer: a cone-producing tree, usually a softwood evergreen (e.g., spruce, pine, fir).

corvid: a member of the crow family (Corvidae); includes crows, jays, magpies and ravens.

covey: a brood or flock of partridges, quails or grouse.

crop: an enlargement of the esophagus; serves as a storage structure and (in pigeons) has glands that produce secretions.

dabbling: a foraging technique used by ducks, where the head and neck are submerged but the body and tail remain on the water's surface; dabbling ducks can usually walk easily on land, can take off without running and have brightly colored speculums.

deciduous tree: a tree that loses its leaves annually (e.g., oak, maple, aspen, birch).

dimorphism: the existence of two distinct forms of a species, such as between the sexes.

eclipse: the dull, female-like plumage that male ducks briefly acquire after molting from their breeding plumage.

elbow patch: a dark spot at the bend of the outstretched wing, seen from below.

flycatching: a feeding behavior where the bird leaves a perch, snatches an insect in mid-air and returns to the same perch; also known as 'hawking' or 'sallying.'

fledgling: a young chick that has just acquired its permanent flight feathers but is still dependent on its parents.

flushing: a behavior where frightened birds explode into flight in response to a disturbance.

gape: the size of the mouth opening.

irruption: a sporadic mass migration of birds into a non-breeding area.

larva: a development stage of an animal (usually an invertebrate) that has a different body form from the adult (e.g., caterpillar, maggot).

leading edge: the front edge of the wing as viewed from below.

litter: fallen plant material, such as twigs, leaves and needles, that forms a distinct layer above the soil, especially in forests.

lore: the small patch between the eye and the bill.

molting: the periodic replacement of worn out feathers (usually once or twice a year).

morphology: the science of form and shape.

nape: the back of the neck.

neotropical migrant: a bird that nests in North America but overwinters in the New World tropics.

niche: an ecological role filled by a species.

open country: a landscape that is primarily not forested.

parasitism: a relationship between two species where one benefits at the expense of the other.

phylogenetics: a method of classifying organisms that puts together groups that share a common ancestry.

pishing: making a sound to attract birds by saying *pishhh* as loudly and as wetly as possible.

polygynous: having a mating strategy where one male breeds with several females.

polyandrous: having a mating strategy where one female breeds with several males.

plucking post: a perch habitually used by an accipiter for plucking feathers from its prey.

raptor: a carnivorous (meat-eating) bird; includes eagles, hawks, falcons and owls.

rufous: rusty red in color.

speculum: a brightly colored patch in the wings of many dabbling ducks.

squeaking: making a sound to attract birds by loudly kissing the back of the hand, or by using a specially design squeaky bird call.

talons: the claws of birds of prey.

understory: the shrub or thicket layer beneath a canopy of trees.

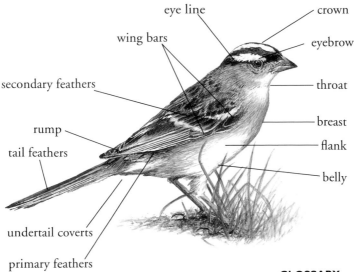

eye line

crown

wing bars

eyebrow

secondary feathers

throat

breast

rump

flank

tail feathers

belly

undertail coverts

primary feathers

References

American Ornithologists' Union. 1983–97. *Check-list of North American Birds.* 6th ed. (and its supplements). American Ornithologists' Union, Washington, D.C.

Bird Observer. 1994. *A Birder's Guide to Eastern Massachusetts.* American Birding Association, Colorado Springs, CO.

DeGraaf, R.M., and J.H. Rappole. 1995. *Neotropical Migratory Birds: Natural History, Distribution, and Population Change.* Cornell University Press, Ithaca, New York.

Ehrlich, P.R., D.S. Dobkin and D. Wheye. 1988. *The Birder's Handbook.* Fireside, New York.

Evans, H.E. 1993. *Pioneer Naturalists: The Discovery and Naming of North American Plants and Animals.* Henry Holt and Company, New York.

Farrand, J., ed. 1983. *The Audubon Society Master Guide to Birding.* 3 vols. Alfred A. Knopf, New York.

Gotch, A.F. 1981. *Birds: Their Latin Names Explained.* Blandford Press, Dorset, England.

Griggs, J.L. 1997. *American Bird Conservancy's Field Guide to All the Birds of North America.* Harper Collins Publishers, New York.

Kaufman, K. 1996. *Lives of North American Birds.* Houghton Mifflin Company, New York.

Mearns, B., and R. Mearns. 1992. *Audubon to Xantus: The Lives of Those Commemorated in North American Bird Names.* Academic Press, San Diego.

Reader's Digest Association. *Book of North American Birds.* The Reader's Digest Association, Pleasantville, New York.

Robbins, C.S., B. Bruun and H.S. Zim. 1966. *Birds of North America.* Golden Press, New York.

Scott, S.S. 1987. *Field Guide to the Birds of North America.* National Geographic Society, Washington, D.C.

Terres, J.K. 1995. *The Audubon Society Encyclopedia of North American Birds.* Wings Books, New York.

Veit, R.R., and W.R. Petersen. 1993. *Birds of Massachusetts.* Massachusetts Audubon Society, Lincoln.

Checklist of Boston-area Birds

This checklist includes 316 bird species recorded in Boston and the surrounding ocean and inland communities. It was compiled using *A Birder's Guide to Eastern Massachusetts* (Bird Observer 1994), *A Checklist of the Birds of Ipswich River Wildlife Sanctuary* (Massachusetts Audubon Society 1993), *Birds of Massachusetts* (Veit and Petersen 1993) and the *Massachusetts Daily Field Card* (Massachusetts Audubon Society 1984).

Checklist symbols

Seasons

W = Winter (mid-December through February)

Sp = Spring (March through May)

Su = Summer (June through July)

F = Fall (August through early December)

Breeding Status

B = Regular breeder (nests every year)

b = Irregular breeder (nests infrequently; few nesting records)

? = Suspected breeder (no confirmation of nesting)

+ = Former breeder (no nesting records in recent years)

L = Local breeder (restricted to a few locations)

Abundance (in appropriate habitats)

C = Common to abundant (always present in large numbers)

F = Fairly common (always present in moderate to small numbers)

U = Uncommon (usually present in small numbers)

R = Rare (observed in very small numbers, and perhaps not every year)

X = Extremely rare (fewer than 10 recorded sightings during that season)

- = Absent (no recorded sightings)

e = Erratic (can occur in substantially larger or smaller numbers during certain years)

* = Abundant offshore (pelagic)

The species in this checklist are listed in taxonomic order (in accordance with the 41st supplement [July 1997] of the American Ornithologists' Union's *Check-list of North American Birds*). A blank line separates each family of birds. This checklist does not include 'accidental' species (recorded fewer than 10 times ever in our area).

	W	Sp	Su	F
Red-throated Loon	R	F	X	C
Common Loon	U	C	R	C
Pied-billed Grebe	R	U	X	F
Horned Grebe	C	F	-	F
Red-necked Grebe	F	U	-	U
Northern Fulmar	F*	R*	X*	R*
Cory's Shearwater	X*	X*	R*	R*
Greater Shearwater	X*	X*	F*	U*
Sooty Shearwater	X*	X*	U*	U*
Manx Shearwater	X*	X*	U*	U*
Wilson's Storm-Petrel	-	-	X*	F*
Leach's Storm-Petrel	-	X*	R*	R*
Northern Gannet	R*	U*	X*	F*
Great Cormorant (b)	Ce	U	R	U
Double-crested Cormorant (B)	X	C	C	C
American Bittern (+)	Re	U	R	U
Least Bittern (bL)	-	R	R	R
Great Blue Heron	Re	F	C	C
Great Egret (bL)	-	U	F	U
Snowy Egret (BL)	-	C	C	C
Little Blue Heron (bL)	-	Ue	Ue	Ue
Tricolored Heron	-	R	R	R
Cattle Egret	-	R	U	R
Green Heron (BL)	-	U	F	U
Black-crowned Night-Heron (BL)	X	U	F	U
Yellow-crowned Night Heron	-	R	R	R
Glossy Ibis (BL)	-	U	U	U
Turkey Vulture	X	U	R	U
Snow Goose	R	U	-	U
Canada Goose (B)	C	C	C	C
Brant	F	F	-	F
Mute Swan	U	U	U	U
Tundra Swan	R	-	-	R
Wood Duck (B)	X	F	F	C
Gadwall	R	F	R	U
Eurasian Wigeon	X	X	-	R
American Wigeon	R	U	-	F
American Black Duck (B)	C	C	U	C
Mallard (B)	C	C	C	C

	W	Sp	Su	F
Blue-winged Teal	-	F	R	F
Northern Shoveler	-	F	-	U
Northern Pintail	-	F	-	F
Green-winged Teal	-	F	X	C
Canvasback	F	U	-	U
Redhead	U	R	-	R
Ring-necked Duck	R	U	-	F
Greater Scaup	F	F	-	F
Lesser Scaup	R	R	-	U
King Eider	R	R	-	R
Common Eider (bL)	C	F	R	F
Harlequin Duck	U	R	-	R
Surf Scoter	U	U	-	F
White-winged Scoter	C	U	-	C
Black Scoter	U	F	-	F
Oldsquaw	F	C	-	C
Bufflehead	C	F	-	F
Common Goldeneye	C	F	-	F
Barrow's Goldeneye	U	R	-	-
Hooded Merganser	F	F	-	F
Red-breasted Merganser (bL)	C	C	X	C
Common Merganser	C	F	-	F
Ruddy Duck	R	R	-	F
Osprey	-	U	-	U
Bald Eagle	F	R	X	R
Northern Harrier	-	R	-	R
Sharp-shinned Hawk	R	U	-	U
Cooper's Hawk	R	R	X	R
Northern Goshawk	R	R	-	R
Red-shouldered Hawk (B)	R	U	R	U
Broad-winged Hawk (B)	-	F	R	F
Red-tailed Hawk (B)	C	F	R	F
Rough-legged Hawk	Ue	Ue	-	Ue
Golden Eagle	R	X	-	R
American Kestrel (B)	U	F	R	F
Merlin	X	U	-	F
Peregrine Falcon (BL)	-	R	R	U
Gyrfalcon	X	-	-	-
Ring-necked Pheasant (B)	R	R	R	R
Ruffed Grouse (B)	R	R	R	R
Wild Turkey (BL)	R	R	R	R
Northern Bobwhite (B)	R	U	U	U
Clapper Rail (BL)	-	R	R	R
King Rail	X	R	X	R

	W	Sp	Su	F
Virginia Rail (BL)	X	U	U	R
Sora (BL)	X	U	R	U
Common Moorhen (BL)	-	X	-	X
American Coot (bL)	U	R	-	F
Sandhill Crane	-	X	-	X
Black-bellied Plover	R	C	R	C
American Golden-Plover	-	R	-	Ue
Semipalmated Plover	-	F	-	C
Piping Plover (BL)	-	R	U	R
Killdeer (B)	-	C	F	C
American Oystercatcher (BL)	-	R	R	R
American Avocet	-	-	-	X
Greater Yellowlegs	-	C	-	C
Lesser Yellowlegs	-	F	-	C
Solitary Sandpiper	-	F	-	F
Willet (BL)	-	F	F	F
Spotted Sandpiper (B)	-	F	R	F
Upland Sandpiper (BL)	-	R	R	R
Whimbrel	-	R	-	F
Hudsonian Godwit	-	-	-	U
Marbled Godwit	-	-	-	R
Ruddy Turnstone	-	U	-	F
Red Knot	-	U	-	C
Sanderling	R	C	R	C
Semipalmated Sandpiper	-	C	X	C
Western Sandpiper	-	-	-	U
Least Sandpiper	-	C	X	C
White-rumped Sandpiper	-	F	-	C
Baird's Sandpiper	-	-	-	R
Pectoral Sandpiper	-	U	-	U
Purple Sandpiper	F	F	-	U
Dunlin	R	F	-	C
Curlew Sandpiper	-	X	-	X
Stilt Sandpiper	-	-	-	U
Buff-breasted Sandpiper	-	-	-	R
Ruff	-	X	-	X
Short-billed Dowitcher	-	F	R	C
Long-billed Dowitcher	-	X	-	F
Common Snipe (?L)	X	Fe	X	Fe
American Woodcock (B)	-	F	R	R
Wilson's Phalarope	-	R	R	R
Red-necked Phalarope	-	R*	-	U*
Red Phalarope	X	R*	-	U*

	W	Sp	Su	F
Great Skua	-	-	-	R*
South Polar Skua	-	-	X*	-
Pomarine Jaeger	-	X*	-	U*
Parasitic Jaeger	-	R*	-	U*
Long-tailed Jaeger	-	-	-	X*
Laughing Gull (?L)	-	C	C	C
Little Gull	-	R*	-	R*
Black-headed Gull	F	U	X	R
Bonaparte's Gull	U	C	F	C
Ring-billed Gull	C	C	C	C
Herring Gull (BL)	C	C	C	C
Iceland Gull	F	R	X	R
Lesser Black-backed Gull	R	R	-	R
Glaucous Gull	U	R	-	R
Great Black-backed Gull (BL)	C	C	C	C
Black-legged Kittiwake	U*	R*	-	F*
Sabine's Gull	-	-	-	R*
Caspian Tern	-	X	-	Re
Royal Tern	-	-	R	-
Roseate Tern (BL)	-	F	R	F
Common Tern (BL)	-	F	F	F
Arctic Tern (BL)	-	U*	U*	U*
Forster's Tern	-	-	-	R
Least Tern (BL)	-	R	U	R
Black Tern	-	R	-	U
Black Skimmer	-	R	R	R
Dovekie	Re*	-	-	-
Common Murre	R*	-	-	-
Thick-billed Murre	R*	-	-	-
Razorbill	U*	-	-	-
Black Guillemot	F*	-	-	-
Atlantic Puffin	R*	-	-	-
Rock Dove (B)	C	C	C	C
Mourning Dove (B)	C	C	C	C
Black-billed Cuckoo (B)	-	Re	Re	Re
Yellow-billed Cuckoo (B)	-	Re	Re	Re
Barn Owl (BL)	R	R	R	R
Eastern Screech-Owl (B)	U	U	R	U
Great Horned Owl (B)	R	R	R	R
Snowy Owl	Ue	-	-	-
Barred Owl (+)	R	U	X	R
Long-eared Owl (bL)	R	R	-	R
Short-eared Owl (+)	R	R	-	R

	W	Sp	Su	F
❏ Northern Saw-whet Owl (BL)	R	R	X	R
❏ Common Nighthawk (BL)	-	F	R	F
❏ Whip-poor-will (+)	-	F	R	R
❏ Chimney Swift (B)	-	C	C	U
❏ Ruby-throated Hummingbird	-	U	R	U
❏ Belted Kingfisher (B)	R	F	R	F
❏ Red-headed Woodpecker (bL)	-	X	-	R
❏ Red-bellied Woodpecker (bL)	R	R	R	R
❏ Yellow-bellied Sapsucker	-	U	-	U
❏ Downy Woodpecker (B)	C	C	C	C
❏ Hairy Woodpecker (B)	F	F	U	F
❏ Northern Flicker (B)	R	C	C	C
❏ Pileated Woodpecker (BL)	R	R	R	R
❏ Olive-sided Flycatcher (+)	-	U	-	U
❏ Eastern Wood-Pewee (B)	-	F	R	F
❏ Yellow-bellied Flycatcher	-	R	-	R
❏ Acadian Flycatcher	-	R	-	R
❏ Alder Flycatcher	-	R	-	X
❏ Willow Flycatcher (B)	-	R	U	X
❏ Least Flycatcher	-	U	R	R
❏ Eastern Phoebe (B)	-	F	R	F
❏ Great Crested Flycatcher (B)		F	R	U
❏ Western Kingbird	-	-	-	R
❏ Eastern Kingbird (B)	-	C	F	C
❏ Northern Shrike	Ue	R	-	R
❏ Loggerhead Shrike	-	-	-	X
❏ White-eyed Vireo (+)	-	R	R	R
❏ Blue-headed Vireo	-	U	-	U
❏ Yellow-throatedVireo (+)	-	R	R	R
❏ Warbling Vireo (B)	-	C	U	U
❏ Philadelphia Vireo	-	R	-	R
❏ Red-eyed Vireo (B)	-	C	U	F
❏ Blue Jay (B)	C	C	C	C
❏ American Crow (B)	C	C	C	C
❏ Fish Crow (BL)	F	F	R	F

	W	Sp	Su	F
❏ Horned Lark	R	R	X	R
❏ Purple Martin (+)	-	R	R	R
❏ Tree Swallow (B)	-	C	C	C
❏ Northern Rough-winged Swallow (B)	-	U	R	R
❏ Bank Swallow	-	F	R	U
❏ Barn Swallow (B)	-	F	C	F
❏ Cliff Swallow	-	U	R	U
❏ Black-capped Chickadee (B)	C	C	C	C
❏ Boreal Chickadee	Re	-	-	-
❏ Tufted Titmouse (B)	F	F	U	F
❏ Red-breasted Nuthatch (BL)	Re	Ue	Re	Fe
❏ White-breasted Nuthatch (B)	F	F	R	F
❏ Brown Creeper (B)	U	U	R	U
❏ Carolina Wren	R	R	R	R
❏ House Wren (B)	-	F	U	F
❏ Winter Wren	Re	U	R	U
❏ Sedge Wren	-	X	X	X
❏ Marsh Wren (BL)	-	F	C	F
❏ Golden-crowned Kinglet	U	F	-	F
❏ Ruby-crowned Kinglet	X	F	-	F
❏ Blue-gray Gnatcatcher (BL)	-	U	R	U
❏ Eastern Bluebird (B)	R	F	U	F
❏ Veery (B)	-	F	U	F
❏ Gray-cheeked Thrush	-	R	-	R
❏ Swainson's Thrush	-	U	-	U
❏ Hermit Thrush (?)	X	F	R	F
❏ Wood Thrush (B)	-	F	R	U
❏ American Robin (B)	U	C	C	C
❏ European Starling (B)	C	C	C	C
❏ Gray Catbird (B)	-	C	C	C
❏ Northern Mockingbird (B)	C	C	C	C
❏ Brown Thrasher (B)	X	U	R	U
❏ American Pipit	-	R	-	F

	W	Sp	Su	F
Cedar Waxwing (B)	R	F	U	F
Blue-winged Warbler	-	F	R	U
Golden-winged Warbler	-	R	X	X
Tennessee Warbler	-	U	-	U
Orange-crowned Warbler	Re	R	-	R
Nashville Warbler (bL)	-	F	X	U
Northern Parula	-	F	-	U
Yellow Warbler (B)	-	C	C	C
Chestnut-sided Warbler (B)	-	F	R	U
Magnolia Warbler	-	F		U
Cape May Warbler	-	R	-	R
Black-throated Blue Warbler	-	F	-	U
Yellow-rumped Warbler	F	C	-	C
Black-throated Green Warbler (?)	-	F	R	U
Blackburnian Warbler	-	U	-	R
Pine Warbler (BL)	-	U	R	R
Prairie Warbler (B)	-	F	R	R
Palm Warbler	-	F	-	F
Bay-breasted Warbler	-	U	-	U
Blackpoll Warbler	-	C	-	C
Cerulean Warbler	-	R	-	X
Black-and-white Warbler (BL)	-	F	R	F
American Redstart (B)	-	C	R	F
Prothonotary Warbler (bL)	-	X	-	X
Worm-eating Warbler (BL)	-	R	X	X
Ovenbird (B)	-	F	R	U
Northern Waterthrush	-	F	-	F
Louisiana Waterthrush	-	R	X	X
Kentucky Warbler	-	X	-	X
Connecticut Warbler	-	-	-	R
Mourning Warbler	-	R	-	R
Common Yellowthroat (B)	-	C	U	C
Hooded Warbler	-	X	-	X
Wilson's Warbler	-	U	-	R
Canada Warbler	-	F	X	R
Yellow-breasted Chat (bL)	-	X	X	R
Summer Tanager	-	X	-	X
Scarlet Tanager (B)	-	F	U	F
Eastern Towhee (B)	-	C	C	F
American Tree Sparrow	C	R	-	R
Chipping Sparrow (B)	-	C	C	F
Field Sparrow (B)	R	F	U	F

	W	Sp	Su	F
Vesper Sparrow	-	R	-	R
Lark Sparrow	-	-	-	X
Savannah Sparrow (BL)	R	F	U	C
Grasshopper Sparrow	-	X	-	X
Saltmarsh Sharp-tailed Sparrow (BL)	X	U	U	F
Nelson's Sharp-tailed Sparrow	R	R	-	R
Seaside Sparrow	-	R	-	R
Fox Sparrow	X	Ue	-	Ue
Song Sparrow (B)	C	C	C	C
Lincoln's Sparrow	-	R	-	R
Swamp Sparrow (B)	U	C	U	C
White-throated Sparrow	F	C	-	C
White-crowned Sparrow	Xe	Ue	-	Ue
Dark-eyed Junco	C	C	-	C
Lapland Longspur	R	-	-	U
Snow Bunting	R	-	-	F
Northern Cardinal (B)	C	C	C	C
Rose-breasted Grosbeak (B)	-	C	U	F
Indigo Bunting (B)	-	F	U	F
Bobolink	-	C	U	C
Red-winged Blackbird (B)	X	C	C	C
Eastern Meadowlark (BL)	R	F	U	F
Rusty Blackbird	-	F	-	F
Common Grackle (B)	X	C	C	C
Brown-headed Cowbird (B)	X	C	R	C
Orchard Oriole (bL)	-	R	X	-
Baltimore Oriole (B)	-	C	R	F
Pine Grosbeak	Xe	-	-	-
Purple Finch (B)	Re	F	R	U
House Finch (B)	C	C	C	C
Red Crossbill	Xe	-	-	-
White-winged Crossbill	Xe	-	-	-
Common Redpoll	Re	-	-	-
Pine Siskin (b)	Ue	Ue	Re	Ue
American Goldfinch (B)	F	C	C	C
Evening Grosbeak	Ue	Ue	-	Ue
House Sparrow (B)	C	C	C	C

Index of Scientific Names

This index references only primary, illustrated species descriptions.

Index of Common Names

Boldface page numbers refer to primary, illustrated species descriptions.

About the Authors

When he's not out watching birds, frogs or snakes, Chris Fisher researches endangered species management and wildlife interpretation at the University of Alberta in Edmonton and serves as president of the local Natural History Club. Chris has traveled throughout North America and Southeast Asia in the pursuit of wild places, and he has produced a series of acclaimed bird guides. By sharing his enthusiasm and passion for wild things through lectures, photographs and articles, Chris strives to foster a greater appreciation for the value of wilderness.

Inspired by wild creatures and wild places, Andy Bezener has developed a keen interest in the study and conservation of birds. Field work with the Canadian Wildlife Service, in addition to studies at Lethbridge Community College and the University of Alberta, has given Andy joyful insight into the lives of many North American birds. His passion and concern for wilderness and wildlife has led him across much of the continent, from the eastern United States to the Queen Charlotte Islands, and from southeastern Arizona to Victoria Island, N.W.T. Through photography, writing, public speaking and travel, he continues to search for a deeper understanding and more meaningful appreciation of nature.